REACHING HOME AT FIRST LIGHT

An Autobiographical Novel

Ron Breazeale, Phd.

Publisher's Name: Ron Breazeale, Phd

ISBN: 978-1-962142-92-2

Contents

Book 2

PART TWO

AT FIRST LIGHT

Lee and Liz finally drifted off to sleep. It took a while. They, like much of the human race that night, weren't sure what was happening. But they tried to have faith that the force that now appeared to be in control of their world was a benevolent one. That what was happening was for good, not evil. Maybe humanity would grow up without destroying itself and the rest of the universe.

CHAPTER 1

Home of Dr. Lee Brazil
Winterpool, Maine
Wednesday, December 15, 2027, 4:13 A.M. EST

It was a very cold February evening. Just before sunset, the sky a crimson red. The sea was calm and still, like a dark sheet of glass that reflected the fading light. The weather was clear. There was no wind. A five-masted schooner, the Carol Deering, *with full sail sat dead in the water, twenty nautical miles southwest of Cape Hatteras. The schooner was en route to Norfolk but carried no cargo.*

One by one, the crew appeared on deck, wordlessly moving toward the lifeboats. Silence hung over the ship. As the Carol Deering *rocked gently, they lowered the lifeboats. They were abandoning ship, but there was no storm. No panic. The schooner wasn't sinking.*

The wheelhouse was already abandoned. The captain was packing his charts and nautical instruments into one of the lifeboats with the assistance of a crewman. The only sounds were the men's footsteps and the sea lapping against the hull of the great schooner.

Off the starboard bow was a bright, metallic blue light. It wasn't the moon, a star, or planet. It wasn't a ship searchlight or a beacon. The color was different, and it hung high above the water, motionless.

A priest in black stood on the bow, mesmerized by the light. A young, blond seaman placed a gold cross with seven green stones that seemed to glow in the priest's right hand. He remained fixated on the light. Another crewman, a black man, silently took him by the arm and led him to a lifeboat. The blond seaman assisted this crewman and the priest into a lifeboat and lowered them into the dark, motionless water.

1

As the first stars of evening appeared, a heavy, gray fog rolled in, first from the West then from the East. One by one, it swallowed the lifeboats. The blond seaman remained on the schooner's deck. His bright green eyes glowed like the stones in the cross as the fog rolled over the Carol Deering.

Lee woke up and rubbed his eyes. He'd had the same dream for the last three nights. When the fog rolled over the schooner, the dream ended and he awoke. He lay back and took a deep breath.

In the last few weeks, for reasons he didn't understand, he'd felt drawn to learn more about the *Carol Deering*. Built in Maine, it was lost in the Bermuda Triangle in 1921. On a cold morning in late February, the five- masted schooner was found grounded on the Diamond Shoals off North Carolina's Outer Banks. When the Coast Guard boarded the schooner, the crew was gone, as were the lifeboats and the captain's instruments and records. It was a ghost schooner. Why it had been abandoned, no one knew. And why Lee had suddenly become so interested in the schooner, he didn't know. But he found himself on websites devoted to the Triangle. He'd depleted the Winterpool Community Library of both its books about Bermuda. And now he'd begun to dream about the ghost schooner. At first, he'd justified these Internet searches because of his concern for a patient, Frank Bowman. Frank had returned to see Lee, complaining of having dreams about the Bermuda Triangle that made no sense to him. But when Lee began having the same dreams, he realized that something else was driving his interest to the point of obsession. He told himself it was just another sign that he was burning out, another indicator that he should get totally out of clinical work. But he knew there was more to it. But what?

Lee turned and tossed for a while and finally managed to doze off. The alarm didn't wake him when it went off at 6:30 A.M. He was late for his first patient.

White's Ferry Road
Winterpool, Maine
Same Day, 3:43 P.M.

Frank had spent most of the day in his office at home. He'd had a terrible night, so he left a note for his wife not to disturb him. She'd tried to talk with him, but he refused to open the door. Finally, she gave up and left to take the children to school and, he assumed, go on to work. His cell phone had rung numerous times that morning, but he hadn't answered. Most of the calls were from her.

Finally, in mid-afternoon he decided to throw some clothes and toiletries into a bag. He'd already called a realtor, as he'd been instructed to do, to rent White's cabin. The realtor had hesitated at first, but she knew Frank. He decided not to wait to explain to his wife what he was doing. He left and drove around until it was close to dark. The realtor had said that she would leave the keys in the mailbox. He'd been adamant with her that he had to be in the cabin by nightfall. He'd called Dr. Brazil's office and left a message, pleading to meet him at the cabin this evening, just as the man in the dream had told him to do. It had all been so clear in the dream, but he was sure that if he told anyone about it, they'd think he was crazy. Maybe even Dr. Brazil would think he was crazy.

He would get to the cabin before dark. He was sure that Dr. Brazil would meet him. Frank was desperate to understand what was happening. The dream kept replaying in his head. There was a ship, a ghost schooner named the *Carol Deering*. A man stood on its deck— an old man with a beard. Frank had never seen him before, but he was speaking directly to Frank. He said his name was Griff, and he told Frank to deliver a message to Dr. Brazil: the doctor would be visited by someone he didn't trust who would ask him for a favor—and he must not refuse. Frank kept hearing the voice in his head. I'm losing my mind, he thought. He was on White's Ferry Road now. The fog was getting thicker, but he was almost there.

Dirt Road
Winterpool, Maine
Same Day, 9:16 P.M.

What distinguishes men from the rest of animals
is his ability to do artificial things.

~ Kurt Vonnegut,

Player Piano

Lee had to concentrate to stay on the road, an especially difficult feat, given that he wanted to think about other things—like Europe and the vacation that he and Liz were planning—not the fog, the road, or the reason he was out in the pucker brush on such a miserable evening.

He hadn't seen Frank Bowman in five years, before he'd shown up at the office two weeks ago, complaining of feeling nervous and anxious and having sleep problems. He wanted to talk that day, so Lee arranged an emergency appointment for later in the afternoon. Frank complained about strange dreams about pirates and a lost sea captain. The dreams didn't "make any sense" to him, he said. He was especially upset by one in which a young woman—he remembered her name, Theo—was begging for her life. He remembered that very clearly.

This morning, as Lee was trying to get out the door to the office, the phone rang. Loretta, Lee's receptionist, was calling to tell him that Frank had called his office early this morning. Loretta had come in early to do some filing and had taken the message.

"Frank sounded agitated," she said. Loretta loved to use professional words, like 'labile' and 'agitated.' He said that he would call back but hadn't. He couldn't keep his 6:00 P.M. appointment at the office, because it "wouldn't be safe," but he had to see Lee this evening. It was "urgent." He explained that he was no longer living with his wife and had taken a winter rental near White's Ferry, 629 White's Ferry Road, to be exact. Lee reluctantly agreed to the meeting and told Loretta to call Frank and confirm the time. She told Lee not to rush, that she would "cover for him" if being out late made him late for his first patient at 8:00 the next morning. She'd always been good at that.

It had been a very long day. Lee wasn't in the habit of making house calls, especially at night, but Frank Bowman had seemed terrified to Loretta, and Lee was also feeling very anxious and confused about the case. He had initially tried to help Frank understand the meaning of his dreams, but Frank had shown little interest in such interpretations. To be honest, Lee had been hard-pressed to come up with these explanations, because he didn't understand the dreams' relationship to Frank's life, either. He just knew that something more was going on than Frank watching too many *Pirates of the Caribbean* reruns.

Frank had initially seen Lee five years ago, after the death of a close friend in a strange boating accident in Bermuda. Lee remembered that the friend's body had never been recovered. Frank, in his late forties at the time, had been married for a number of years, happily he said. He had two children and worked in the reinsurance industry, which required him to travel frequently between Portland and Bermuda. Reinsurance companies, Lee had learned from Frank, took risks that most insurance companies wouldn't. They insured the insurance companies. According to Frank, Maine and Bermuda were two of the industry's "hot spots," with most reinsurance companies located in Portland or Hamilton.

"Turn right on Mill Turn Road," said the mechanical voice. Thank God for GPS, thought Lee. He could barely see the road, much less signs.

It started to snow. The roads would freeze soon. "This was a bad idea and getting worse," Lee muttered. "I'm too old for this crap."

He made the turn onto Mill Turn. Snow hadn't been forecasted. When he'd left the office, the sky had been clear, Orion rising in the eastern sky.

"In 300 feet turn right on White's Ferry Road." Lee slowed the car to a crawl. Okay, there it is. I think. He turned.

"Recalculating," said the voice.

"Oh, shut up," groaned Lee. "So, I missed it. Keep your shirt on. I'll turn around." And he did, with some difficulty, and turned again. His wife Liz complained that he wouldn't buy a new smartphone with advanced navigation. But his old smartphone was smart enough. He hated technology, especially new technology. He'd once looked forward to retirement, when he wouldn't have to carry a pager. Well, he didn't have a pager anymore, but smartphones were worse. Why buy something with "advanced features" when he didn't use the basic features he had now? If it ain't broke, why the hell fix it? He knew the answer. Money. Good old capitalism. "Go shopping," George W. had suggested.

"Go .3 miles. 629 White's Ferry Road is on your right."

Lee began to notice that the fog up ahead had a strange orange glow. The combination of fog and snow on the coast in December wasn't unusual, but an orange glow certainly was. As he crept along the road, it seemed to grow brighter and began to mix with blue and red.

His cellphone rang. Now what? He glanced at the number but didn't recognize it. "This is Dr. Brazil." The line was dead. Another dropped call.

Lee glanced back at the road just in time to avoid Rob Daniels. He was standing in the center of the road in his worn-out yellow rain suit, which he wore when he was, as Lee put it, "playing volunteer fireman."

Rob was waving him over to the side of the road. Lee lowered the window. "Jesum, Rob, I almost ran you over. What's up?"

"One doozy of a fire," said Rob with a smile. "I don't think I've seen one like this before."

"Anyone hurt?"

"Dunno, Nothing's left of the place. Just a pile of embers."

"I hope nobody was in there," said Lee, thinking about Frank.

"Melted the damn car. Melted it! Never seen anything like that. Chief hasn't either."

"Where is the Chief?"

"Up there," said Rob, pointing. "Now, you be careful, Doc. There's a lot of . . . strange things going on around here tonight."

"What do you mean . . . strange?"

Rob hesitated. "I don't know, Doc. Things . . . they just aren't right around here tonight," he said, staring into the fog behind Lee's car. Lee waited.

"I don't know, Doc. Just talk to the Chief."

He closed the window and drove slowly through the fog. The Chief's pickup was parked behind other rescue vehicles. He was on his cellphone.

Lee pulled over and got out. He stood back, giving the Chief some privacy while he surveyed the scene. James White's cottage was a pile of ash. Flattened. Lee had seen a lot of burned-out structures over the years with his work with fire and rescue, but never like this. The plumbing, the appliances, everything was melted flat.

Chief Thibodeau was a big man with bright red hair, starting to gray. Clean-shaven, in his late forties. He loved his job but was currently shaking his head. "Damnedest thing I've ever seen." Lee wondered who was on the line. He ended the call and motioned to Lee.

Lee extended his hand. "How are you, Chief?"

"Confused. That was the FBI. Why the hell are they calling me? We just got this call forty-five minutes ago. What are you doing out here?"

Lee hesitated. This was one of those times when he had to decide if it was in a patient's best interest to break confidentiality. Clearly it was.

"I got a call from a patient. He'd just rented this cottage for the winter and said he wanted to meet me here. He was insistent that we meet tonight. But I have no idea what this is about."

"Well, it seems that the Feds knew your patient, Frank. How and why, I don't know. I asked Chief Moore to come out. I told him the police should be involved, since this looks like . . . arson, I suppose." The Chief shook his head again, looking puzzled at the pile of ash that was White's cottage. "I don't know exactly what it looks like."

"Do you think that anyone was in there, Mike?"

"I don't know. It'll take twenty-four hours for this to cool down enough to allow the State Fire Marshal and maybe the Feds to answer that question." He motioned in the direction of the field next to the cottage. "I do have something, though." His voice trailed off.

Through the smoke, Lee could see a couple of firemen standing at the edge of the field with their flashlights.

"Look at this," said the Chief, shining his light across the field. "We put this out when we got here." The snow that had covered the ground had melted. The grass was flattened, singed, and still smoking.

"It's almost a perfect circle," said the Chief. "Probably shouldn't say this to you, Doc; you'll think I'm completely crazy, but the first thing I thought of was those damn crop circles. You know, the pranks those kids in the Midwest pulled to make authorities think there'd been some type of 'alien landing'? If this is a prank, it is a damned elaborate and expensive one. How the hell did they do this?"

"I don't know." Frank had sounded desperate, but Lee didn't think that he would burn down the cottage down. What would be the point? And this business . . . a perfect circle? He scanned it again, as one of the firemen moved his light across the field. "Makes no sense," he said. And it didn't.

Lee stayed for another half hour. There didn't seem to be very much to say or do. No one understood what had happened. When Police Chief Moore arrived, he had no new insights to add.

Condominium of Joann Lawrence
Portland, Maine
Thursday, December 16th, 8:05 A.M.

Joann was straightening up when she noticed that her laptop was on. Strange, she thought. She usually turned it off. As she would say, "Saving power is saving money." But she hadn't had to worry about that since she'd "come into money," as she put it, a few years ago.

She started to turn the computer off but noticed her grandfather's cross on the desk next to the computer. "I must be losing it," she muttered. "How did that get there?" It was a small gold cross, with seven green stones that seem to glow in the early morning light.

She picked up the cross in her right hand, and her left hand seemed to move on its own, scrolling through employment ads for nannies. She stopped on one: "Temporary position on *The Saint*, a luxury cruise liner. Cruise to Bermuda. Six days. Departs Boston December 18th. Returns to Boston December 24th. Assist parents with care of two boys, ages 7 and 9. Competitive wage. Must be experienced, mature, and provide references."

"Hmm," she said with interest, "why not? It would get me out of here for the holidays. I don't need the money, though." A single woman in her mid-sixties, she'd been retired for some time. She continued to talk to herself. "But, what the heck? And I could . . ." she hesitated, ". . . do what I think I should." At least what she'd felt like doing for the last few weeks, since she'd found the cross in an old jewelry box. She hadn't worn it in years, but, for some reason — she couldn't remember what—she'd been going through the jewelry case and saw it. From that moment, she'd felt like she should return it to the Episcopal Church in Bermuda where her grandfather had served as a priest. It puzzled her why she should suddenly feel such a strong desire to do so, but, she thought, I could see the church and some of the island. I've always wanted to see Bermuda. For some reason, she never had.

CHAPTER 2

Lee's Home
Winterpool, Main
Wednesday, December 16th, 1:00 A.M.

Hope: Eating the air on promise of supply.

~ Shakespeare

L ee had gotten home late. Liz was already in bed. He had a restless night. Crop circles, a melted car, a disappearing patient. He needed to get out of this business completely. He kept thinking about the young woman in his patient's dreams. Theo. Pleading for her life.

Theo. Short for Theodosia? Lee slipped out of the bedroom without turning on a light and went into his study. He thumbed through the bookcase and found it. *The Bermuda Triangle* by Adi-Kent Thomas Jeffery. Theodosia was the daughter of Vice President Aaron Burr and the wife of the first governor of South Carolina. She had a tragic history, with her mother having died when she was a young girl and her father being exiled after his fatal duel with Alexander Hamilton. She was on her way from South Carolina to New York City to be reunited with Burr when the small sailing ship she was aboard, *The Patriot*, disappeared in the Triangle.

Go back to sleep, he told himself and finally did around 3:00 A.M. But morning came very quickly. He rolled over and looked out the window of their bedroom. Brown Island Light flashed in the distance. A lobster boat moved across the dark water. To the east, the sky was starting to brighten. Shades of red and orange. The weather was clearing.

It had snowed again in the night. It was still dark, as it always was in December. Lee rolled over again and closed his eyes. Some mornings he woke up with a start, confused, afraid. He understood the power of dreams.

Sometimes they took him back to the gray cell he'd once called home for a year. He'd been released and returned home to Winterpool five years ago. No charges pressed. No apology given. No comment to the press. "Just the way the government wants it," his attorney had said.

Lee's nightmare had begun when he'd returned to the South of his childhood to work on a book about the atomic energy industry. He'd lived near the plants in the 1950s. His father had worked there. Lee had grown up without a left hand, a birth defect. Accidents occurred in those days that no one reported. He was sure that his father had gotten a good dose of something—radiation, mercury? God knows what—before Lee was conceived, and he blamed the atomic energy industry for his birth defect.

He'd been preparing to return to Maine when an accident occurred at one of the Department of Energy plants. A major accident. Lee was caught up in the ensuing chaos and implicated in what the Feds had initially believed was a terrorist attack. He was detained but, with the help of a homeless man, managed to escape from the detention facility. He began his trek home and, along the way, found a number of unlikely allies: A woman trying to run away from the memories of her family and her dead son; a truck driver still fighting the ghosts of Vietnam; and Jean, the lost love of his youth. But before Lee reached home, he was detained again by FBI Agent Jennings, whom Lee described as a "real piece of work," a burnt-out FBI agent and cancer survivor who had a temper and probably drank too much. Even though he was instrumental in Lee's detention, the two developed a strange friendship over the course of time. Lee couldn't think of another word that described the relationship.

Lee's release in the spring of 2024 had been a surprise. He only learned of it when Jennings appeared at the door of his cell late one morning and announced that Lee was going home. Lee had learned not to question good news. He quickly packed his clothes and notes into the two shopping bags that the government had provided and put on the old, gray trench coat and plastic boots that Jennings offered. Jennings then drove him to the train station to catch the Downeaster to Brunswick, Maine.

Lee and Jennings hadn't talked in some time. After the first couple months of his detention, they had little left to say to one another. That morning, an awkward silence had hung over them. Jennings finally broken the silence as they approached North Station.

"You'll remember the agreement we have, won't you?" "It would be hard to forget," said Lee.

"Mum's the word. There'll be no comment from our side, and there'd better be no comment from yours." Jennings stared sharply at Lee.

Lee nodded and mumbled, "Yes, master."

"Well, it's good to see you're still the cynical, sarcastic son of a bitch I've grown to love over the last year," Jennings noted.

Lee smiled and tried to laugh but couldn't. He turned to Jennings. "Well, I appreciate your help in arranging this."

Jennings looked like he wasn't sure what to say. They both seemed uncomfortable as they shook hands. Lee boarded the Downeaster and took a seat by the window, facing forward. He sat by himself. Only a few fares were riding at that time of day.

Since his return, his faith in the U.S. government hadn't been restored. Indeed, the events of the past five years only seemed to further undermine his trust in government—a Congress whose members represented only their own interests and those of large corporations, and politicians who believed that character assassination and mud-slinging was a fine way to conduct the business of the country.

Add to that the exponential growth of technology. Data collection and dissemination systems were far outpacing the abilities of people or governments to monitor and regulate. Lee often thought about his time in detention, but this morning he had no time. He had other things on his mind: A missing patient—where the hell was Frank? And the White's cabin and crop circles—or whatever was in the field. And, of course, all of this was happening before the vacation he'd planned for months. Great timing.

The alarm sounded as Lee was shaving—he'd forgotten to switch it off. He was almost always awake before it rang, but he needed to get up early this morning. Most mornings he didn't. Not since his daughter had started driving herself to school in the old Subaru that Lee and Liz had bought for her in her senior year in high school. And since he'd retired—well, semi- retired—he didn't need to be in the office until 10:00. But old habits die hard; he was usually there between 7:30 and 8:00 A.M.

Liz was still asleep, as she was most mornings when he left. Lee always showered and shaved in the morning: the same routine he'd followed for most of his life. He hated eating alone, but most mornings he did. A breakfast of high-fiber, cardboard-flavored cereal. It was boring, but so were a lot of his meals. He tried now more than ever to watch his diet. He had developed high blood pressure while in detention and had been taking medication since his return. As he finished the last of the bran cereal, he paged through *Time Magazine*. Thank God they were still printing it. He remembered what happened to *Newsweek*.

There was an article about Beta 17 and TransSea's plan to mine the asteroid. About the size of Delaware, Beta 17 was part of the asteroid belt. Astronomers had discovered it in 1992, and it was now hurtling toward a close encounter with Earth. A collision would, of course, result in the extinction of life as we know it. But readers were assured that this was not going to happen. At least not this time. Beta 17 would pass very, very close to Earth, within just nine-hundred and fifty thousand miles, and TransSea, an "Energy

Corporation," would take this opportunity to launch a mining probe that would land on the asteroid to take core samples from the rock's crust. Observations made by another TransSea probe suggested that the asteroid contained very rare minerals that were becoming depleted on Earth as the number of electronic devices manufactured and used increased exponentially. The asteroid's closest approach to the Earth would occur during the first week of January.

He also saw articles about the Democratic presidential challenger, Senator Clayton. This time, Democrats seemed united—a rarity. He'd give the lady credit. If she could get Democrats to stop fighting with each other, she must have something going for her. Hopefully, this time wouldn't be a disaster, like 2016.

"All right, I'm out of here," Lee said to an empty room. He headed up the stairs to kiss his wife goodbye. Liz was just opening her eyes.

"Hey, lady, how are you doing this morning?" Lee said, trying to sound cheerful.

"Tired. I didn't sleep that well. I don't know what I'm going to do on this trip."

"It'll be fine," said Lee.

Liz rolled over and closed her eyes. "Lee, how many times do I have to tell you that saying things like that isn't helpful?"

"Oh," said Lee, with a shrug and a smile, "probably a few hundred more."

"What time will you be home?"

"I should be out of the office by three or three thirty. I'll see you by four. We'll figure out dinner. And I'm sure you've got more packing to do." He smiled and kissed her. He always kissed her.

The wind was up again, blowing from the north, but the snow had stopped. He opened the garage door and backed the car with some difficulty onto the street. His driveway hadn't been plowed yet, and the city, as usual, had plowed him in.

"Another day in paradise," mumbled Lee, laughing to himself. He frequently laughed at his own jokes.

CHAPTER 3

Winterpool, Maine
Thursday, December 16th, 8:28 A.M.

Lee didn't stop for coffee. He'd given up the habit a year before. Well, not completely. Most days, he white-knuckled it past his favorite coffee stop. He'd given up a lot of his bad habits. Unfortunately, this change usually didn't make Fridays any easier. The energy and excitement he might have felt for the week on Tuesday were usually gone by Thursday afternoon. On Friday, he often felt like Mark Twain's sinking ship. He had no more cargo left to throw overboard.

Lee checked his service. No calls. He called Chief Moore. "So, what's going on out there?"

"Sorry, Doc, nothing to report. No one's seen your guy. His family is in the dark as well. Haven't seen him or his car since late yesterday. Who knows? Maybe he's got a girlfriend we don't know about."

"Well, maybe," said Lee, sounding a little disgusted with the whole matter. "Anything from the State or the Feds?"

"The fire marshal doesn't think that anyone was in the cottage. Of course, that's hard to say for sure, given . . . well, you saw it. And the Feds, as usual, aren't telling me anything. I'll call you once I hear something."

"Good, good," Lee said absently and hung up. "Well," he muttered, "nothing else to do but wait." He continued conversing with himself. "I hate leaving things this way, but I'll be damned if I'm going to change our plans again." Lee and Liz had put off going three times—for Liz's surgery, the flooded basement, and an airline strike.

But not this time. He hadn't been to Europe in years. It was only a week; they wanted to be back to spend Christmas with their daughter Dru and her boyfriend Rob. Their relationship was starting to look serious. Lee had mixed feelings about that. Grandchildren had always felt like a nice idea. But maybe it was too late. She was in her late 30s. They could adopt. But "giving away" his only daughter? She was a young, independent woman now, her own person, and would, as Liz reminded him, decide to what and to whom *she* gave herself.

Lee's resolve on this Friday was to just get to mid-afternoon and leave. He had a light day. Mostly paperwork and phone calls. He did, however, have to get through a two-hour supervision session with Erica, a young psychologist just finishing her requirements for licensure. And, of course, there was lunch with Rick.

As he pulled into the office parking lot, he was reminded that most of his colleagues were considerably younger than he was. There were a lot of hybrids in the lot now. Roger's old Jeep was gone, and so was Roger, traveling in Europe. Bill's Volvo wasn't there, either. He was off sailing somewhere. Most of the old crew had retired. Just Lee and a few others, like Rick Forester, remained. He'd almost forgotten about Rick, but, unfortunately, that was usually impossible. Rick had insisted on taking him to lunch before he left for his trip. A lunch with Rick usually meant that he was in some kind of trouble.

Lee drove into the space closest to the building. Although he was no longer managing the practice, he'd retained the best parking space. His "time away" had been reason enough to hand over the responsibilities of management to someone else, but, it had also been time to do so. He had little interest in continuing to deal with the day-to-day problems of running a clinical practice.

His office was in an old farmhouse built just after the Civil War. The therapists and their clients felt comfortable there. But it was an old building, constantly needing something.

And then there were the clinicians. Overall, a good-hearted and competent lot, but all independent practitioners, so they worked for themselves; set their own hours; and, as they frequently pointed out, decided what they would and wouldn't do. Getting them to move together on anything was like herding cats.

Last of all was Loretta, the receptionist and office manager: A short, stocky woman, under five feet, with frizzy black-from-a-bottle hair; a woman of unknown age. Lee was sure that she was in her late seventies or early eighties. She and her husband had run a bed and breakfast up the coast, but it took at least two people to make it work, so she gave it up when her husband died and came to work for the practice.

Loretta ran a tight ship. Work meant seven each morning, organized, and focused. Disorganization and Dr. Forester, often one in the same, drove her crazy. She still looked to Lee for direction, even though Jim Hardy was officially in charge. She was one of the few who still did. Dr. Hardy's star was rising and Lee's was setting.

"Dr. Brazil, the Internet's out again, and most of the clinicians are complaining that their cell phones aren't working as they should."

"I'm sorry, Loretta. I don't know what to tell you. That's Dr. Hardy's department; you need to talk with him."

"And the land-lines aren't working right, either. I don't know what's going on."

"No one does, Loretta. The paper this morning said something about increased solar activity. Is Dr. Hardy in yet?"

"No. He won't be in till noon."

Lee thought for a moment. Should he? No! "Loretta, I'm sorry, but there's really not much I can do about this. I'll talk to Jim when he arrives and see that he gets on it." And with that, Lee started up the stairs to his second-floor office.

The centerpiece of the office was a small, painted fireplace, an "Italian fireplace" the realtor had called it when Lee had bought the place forty years before. He'd used it frequently in the early years of the practice, but it hadn't seen a fire in a while. Like a lot of things now, Lee felt that it wasn't worth the bother.

The room was large, with tall Victorian windows and a tin ceiling, all original. Overstuffed bookcases lined the walls. Awards, plaques, and a couple of prints from local artists of the North Atlantic covered the wallpaper that Lee had never liked. An old couch from his practice in Tennessee took up most of the space on another wall. He'd kept it, though he doubted that it was comfortable; his clients preferred his grandfather's old rocker or the Swedish recliner he used for teaching relaxation exercises. Lee settled into the work of the day. He made a few phone calls and began plodding through case reviews and sign-offs with Erica.

As he did, he thought of the past. He could remember when he and his office manager installed the first PCs for word processing and billing. Before iPads, smartphones, and the newest "must have" mini micro-widget that did unnecessary things.

The practice of psychology was now heavily "evidence based," meaning that all therapy should be based on research evidence. Lee had no problem with the concept but felt that much of the "new psychology" was pseudo- science, just like medicine. Blinking lights and numbers didn't make something a science. Lee still believed that psychotherapy was more art than science, a view no longer in vogue in the profession. He also thought that healing resided in the relationship between therapist and patient, not in an algorithm. Lee had always worried about attaching a number to a person, such as a diagnostic code like 309.4, which might give clinicians a false sense of confidence in what they were doing.

Psychologists would soon be licensed to prescribe psychotropic medications in Maine. Licensing had changed in eight other states, almost all rural, that had a shortage of well-trained psychiatrists. Although Lee supported the movement, he was concerned about the impact on the profession. Writing a scrip was indeed easier than helping people learn to deal with painful issues in their lives in a new way. He worried that, like psychiatrists, many psychologists might do what was easiest instead of what was best for the patient.

"Dr. Brazil, you'll need to sign off on this one, too."

"Yes, of course," he answered automatically, still lost in thought.

Dr. Erica Bowdin was slim and attractive, with blue eyes and blond hair tied back. Fit. She listened to Lee's suggestions and direction, although he doubted that she frequently agreed with him. She was a bright and articulate woman from a family with money—the money to send her to the right schools. She was in the vanguard of the new psychology. Leading the charge. Jim and others were pleased that she'd decided to join the practice.

"Well, Dr. Brazil," she was still uneasy calling him Lee, "looking forward to your trip? I was in London and Paris late last fall. Paris is such a special place."

Lee was now the one feeling uneasy. "Well, yes, it is, isn't it?" He wasn't about to tell her that he hadn't been to either special place in years. "It'll be a short visit. I wish it were longer," he said as he moved toward his office door and opened it.

She followed. "Well, enjoy," she said.

"I will."

Lee looked at his watch and remembered lunch with Rick. He grimaced, wondering what Rick had gotten himself into this time. Rick was a colleague and, yes, a friend, although Lee seldom saw him outside of work. He'd worked in the practice for the last ten years. He was a psychiatrist in his early sixties and semi-retired, although not by choice.

Rick's reputation among his colleagues had suffered numerous blows while Lee was away. He'd gotten himself into trouble with the Board. Nothing too egregious: inappropriate comments about his personal life to a patient. God knows, his personal life was a mess and had been for years. Twice divorced, he paid alimony and supported children he never saw.

But today Lee decided to take a pass on Dr. Forester. He would let Dr. Hardy worry about whatever there was to worry about.

As Lee started down the stairs, he heard Rick's door open.

"Lee, wait up."

"I'm sorry, Rick, I just can't do lunch today. Too much to do before I leave. We'll have lunch when I get back. If you need something from the practice, talk with Hardy." Lee didn't wait for a response. He turned and headed for his car. He quickly opened the door, started the engine, and pulled out. He'd escaped. He was on Forest Street.

The Forum, he thought. I can check on Ken, too. It was just a few blocks from the office. It was a nice place, with white tablecloths and candles. Great for a night out, but a little strange for lunch in Winterpool.

Marie, a woman in her late forties, with long brown hair and bright brown eyes, was working behind the take-out counter. Lee ordered a gyro. He could eat it and continue to proof the reports that needed to go out before he left. Joey, Marie's son, began to prepare the sandwich.

"Well, how's he doing?" asked Lee.

"Oh, your boy? He's doing fine. He's a hard worker. Come see," said Marie, as she moved toward the door to the kitchen.

Lee followed. Marie opened the door.

"Kenny," she said, "Doc's here to see you."

Ken was a big man in his late thirties. His size, combined with his temper, had frightened people and limited where he could live and work. In recent years, however, with Lee's help, he'd gotten his temper under control. He'd lived at home all his life, until just a few months ago when he moved into a group home. The job in the restaurant, which Lee had helped arrange, started a few days ago. Steve had a soft spot for guys like Ken. Steve and Marie gave him the title of sous chef and general assistant to the executive chef, Steve.

Ken looked up and smiled. "Doc, when are you starting on that new book?"

Lee returned the smile. "Soon. Why don't you give me a call and we'll talk about it? Looks like you're doing a great job."

"I hope so," said Ken with indecision in his voice. "I really want to." Steve, who was leaning over a pot of something that smelled wonderful, joined the conversation. "He is. But we're not paying him to chit-chat with the likes of you, Doc."

"Okay, okay," said Lee. "You call me, Ken."

"I . . . I will."

"How's your hand?"

"Fine," said Ken, trying to ignore the question to continue working.

"Okay," Lee replied, closing the door to the kitchen.

Ken had been attacked by a couple of local kids. Marie called them thugs. They targeted people who were a little different. But Ken, a wrestling fan who'd been studying the martial art Kali, carried the day and sent the two running for home. Unfortunately, he'd broken a finger in the scuffle.

"I called their parents, Doc, and told them that those kids had better leave my Kenny alone or they'll wish they had," said Marie.

"You tell 'em. Thanks, Marie. I appreciate you guys."

When Lee pulled into the office parking lot, he could see Loretta standing just inside the door. She was waiting for him. Something was wrong. She was talking to herself.

Lee opened the office door, and Loretta turned the conversation she was having with herself toward him. "I couldn't stop them."

"What are you talking about, Loretta? Slow down."

But her agitation was increasing. "They're in your office!"

"Who's in my office?"

"Two men from the government. They showed me their . . . well, I don't know what they showed me. They said it would be better if they waited in your office."

Loretta started to cry, which really didn't require much since her son's accident a few months ago.

The waiting room was empty. Lee moved past Loretta. "It's okay, Loretta. Just calm down. I'm sure it'll be okay," he said over his shoulder as he started up the stairs.

Lee's office door was ajar. He pushed it open with force.

"Come in, Dr. Brazil, and close the door," said a familiar voice.

CHAPTER 4

Winterpool, Maine
Thursday, December 16th, 12:52 P.M.

When you're going through hell, keep going.

~ Winston Churchill

Lee stared blankly at the door latch, hoping that the voice would slide back into the past. It didn't.

"I knew you'd be surprised. But in life, one never knows what's around the next corner. Right, Doc? I think you told me that once."

Lee turned slowly to face Special Agent Jennings. He was seated at Lee's desk in the old and now quite dilapidated brown leather chair Lee had bought when he'd begun his practice in Winterpool.

Lee tried to compose his thoughts. "So, what brings you to Winterpool?" he asked, his voice cracking.

"I like a man who gets down to business. Don't you agree, Andrew?"

"Does this have anything to do . . ."

Jennings interrupted. "No, nothing to do with last night."

"How . . ." Lee stopped himself.

"Well, first things first. This is Andrew Smith, an old friend of mine who works for our government."

"Call me Andy," he said as he stood and extended his hand. Andy smiled. Lee didn't. Lee gave his hand a weak shake.

Andrew, Lee thought, looked like an aging Howdy Doody.

"So, let me ask again. Why are you and Andrew—Andy—here?"

"We need . . ."

"My help." Lee finished his sentence.

"Exactly," said Jennings.

Lee cringed. He was sure that his reaction was clear to his two guests.

"Just a small favor," said Jennings, smiling.

"How small?" Lee asked with obvious irritation.

"We need you to pick something up and deliver it for us."

"Why not UPS or FedEx? I know the government is trying to control spending but . . ."

"Doc, you're still the smartass I learned to love years ago. You're leaving for London tomorrow evening, and then you have a meeting in Paris on Tuesday and back to the States on Thursday, Christmas Eve."

Lee was a bit surprised that Jennings knew his travel plans, though he knew the Feds had monitored his activities closely since his release. Still, it was a jolt.

"Your travel plans fit well with our needs," said Jennings.

"And what, specifically, are your needs?"

"We've needed someone, or I should say Andrew has needed someone, planning a trip like yours for a long time."

Lee remembered that Liz had booked their tickets months before. Liz would stay in London and visit friends from Leister, who would come down for last-minute Christmas shopping, and Lee would go to Paris on the Eurostar. He'd wanted to take the train since it was completed. He would attend a day-long conference by the World Health Organization on health promotion and wellness and write the whole thing off as a business trip.

"It needs to be somebody they wouldn't suspect of working with us," said Andrew.

"Of working with you?"

"Yes, with the United States government."

Lee remembered his first encounter with someone from the U.S. government, aka the CIA, looking for a psychologist to work with retired agents. Over the next two years, Lee had gotten a few mysterious referrals of people who'd also "worked for the U. S. government."

"So, it can't be one of your agents."

"Exactly," said Jennings.

"What's this 'something' you want me to pick up?" asked Lee.

Jennings turned to Andrew, who responded with hesitation. "Let's just say that it belongs to us, and we need to get it into safe hands."

Here we go again, thought Lee.

"How many lives are at stake this time?" asked Lee sarcastically.

"Look, Doc, this is serious business," said Jennings, with some force and irritation.

"I'm sure it is, but you have people who do this sort of thing, don't you? Why don't you use one of them?"

"Well, we've had some trouble at our Paris station," answered Andrew, looking away from Lee. "Let's just say that there are some problems with doing it that way."

Lee turned to Jennings. "Do I have a choice about this?"

Jennings smiled broadly. "Well, not really, unless you want to spend some more time with us in Boston. We discussed this years ago, before your release. Have you forgotten our conversation at North Station?"

"I've tried to."

Andrew made eye contact with Lee. "You'd be doing the government a great service. It's taken years to develop this project. We don't want it compromised."

"So, what do I pick up, and where do I pick it up and drop it off?

"Relax, Doc. They'll give you the details once you're in London. You'll be staying at the Thistle Marble Arch, right?"

"Yes, I think so."

Jennings' smile was cunning. "So, we have a deal. Don't worry. It's a slam dunk. Be over in a few days."

Lee recalled that these were the CIA director's famous last words before the invasion of Iraq. But Lee didn't say anything else.

Jennings got to his feet, as did Andrew. "Good to see you again, Doc.

We'll let you get back to work."

"I'll see you in Paris, Dr. Brazil," said Andrew.

And with that, they were gone.

Lee closed the door and sat down on the couch. He'd hoped he would never see Jennings again. His mind flashed back to the last days in Boston before his release. The small cell in which he'd spent months, the heavy metal doors, the window that looked onto the bay. The sounds. The smells.

The intercom buzzed. Lee sprang to his feet.

"Yes, Loretta, they've gone . . . just some questions about my last tax return. We got it all straightened out. Everything is fine."

Loretta didn't sound convinced, but Lee wouldn't say more. He'd be back in a week, and Jennings would be, once again, in the past Hopefully.

Loretta did have some good news: "Frank Bowman called to apologize for last night. He said that he'd be out of town for the next few days and would call for an appointment when he returned. He didn't leave a number." Lee hadn't been able to reach him on his cell.

"And Chief Moore called. Frank called and told him that he knew about the fire, but he hadn't yet moved his stuff into the cottage. He said that he'd come by the station when he got back. Chief Moore wasn't sure where he was calling from."

Lee felt some relief. False alarm, just like all the other false alarms he'd dealt with over the years. But just like at the fire department, they all had to be answered.

He forced himself to make the last few phone calls of the day. He finished the last report. He would be gone for only a few days, but now it seemed much longer. He called the answering service to give them his contact information and left a note about one of his patients for the on- call clinician. Finally, he left a brief voicemail for Hardy about Dr. Forester.

Lee locked his office door and said good-bye to Loretta, wishing her happy holidays, even though he knew the holidays would be a struggle for her. She missed her husband, especially around the holidays, although she would never admit to or talk about it. Perhaps most difficult for her was her son's slow recovery from the car accident. He would be spending the holidays at a Portland rehab center. Lee thought of what Loretta would say when anyone showed concern or sympathy for her: "Such is life."

Lee buttoned his overcoat and put on the gray flannel hat that he started wearing this time of year. He scanned the reception area and the waiting room one last time. His old leather briefcase felt relatively light; he wasn't taking work with him. He opened the door and stepped out into the late afternoon twilight. The wind was cold and off the ocean.

CHAPTER 5

Paraway Beach Road
Winterpool, Maine
Thursday, December 16th, 3:49 P.M.

Home was only a few minutes away. It was a set on a rise with a view of the open ocean. It was beautiful, but, like the office, it was old and always had something to repair. They'd tried to sell it, but with the recession it hadn't been possible. Liz owned a "camp" inland that they'd turned it into a country house over the years. She loved it. Her studio was there. She would stay there all the time if she could, but Lee couldn't or wouldn't commute three days a week. He was going to quit soon. Completely. Then they would rent the ocean house if they couldn't sell it.

Lee decided to take the long way home, via Paraway Beach. He just wanted to look at the North Atlantic for a few minutes. It was four in the afternoon, but the sun was low. It would be dark when he arrived home. He switched on Maine Public Radio. The four o'clock news had just finished, and MPR was beginning a special report on the Supercomputer. Lee focused his attention on the newscast.

"Jim, we've been hearing a lot about this Supercomputer that the European Union has been working on for the last few years."

"Yes, but they have apparently run out of money and are turning over the final phase of development to the United States government."

"And that's stirred up considerable controversy, hasn't it?"

"It has, indeed, and Senator Nancy Clayton is at the center of it. Here is an address she made to the Senate in late October regarding S126, a Bill to Develop and Expand Information Technology for the Next Generation":

"Let me say first, I'm not against the development of new technologies as many have accused me of being. What I am opposed to is the development of new technology without a clear and reasoned understanding as to its impact on our world. The present bill before the Senate, as I understand it, would assure the continued development of an ultra-intelligent computer. This machine could design even smarter machines and create what British mathematician I.J. Good described as an 'intelligence explosion,' that could leave human intelligence far behind.

"Such a computer would extend our intellectual abilities in the same way that cars and planes have extended our physical abilities. It could develop new treatments for disease and the negative effects of old age. We might even find ways to extend life indefinitely. And the entire universe could open up to exploration . . . and possible exploitation."

Lee was remembering the well-known science-fiction novelist Vernor Vinge, who, in the early 1990s, proposed that humanity would have the means to create superhuman intelligence within thirty years. He also predicted that, shortly afterward, the "human era" would end. He was referring to the coming technological Singularity. Lee refocused on the Senator's speech to Congress.

"The word 'Singularity' is borrowed from astrophysics and refers to a point in space and time, for example, inside a black hole, where the rules of ordinary physics no longer apply. I would ask what rules will apply if we choose to develop this ultra-intelligent machine? How will we chart our course? If we apply only the rules of finance and profit, we could enter a black hole from which our world will never emerge.

"Therefore, I encourage this body to consider an amendment to the present bill that would create a commission composed of our best minds and hearts to explore the moral implications of developing this new technology and to provide guidance to those who would create it. I am submitting such an amendment, and I hope that this body will give it serious consideration and act on it favorably."

The commentator continued. "Jim, I understand that the amendment introduced by Senator Clayton and co-sponsored by a number of senators did not pass."

"Yes, it was defeated soundly by a vote of sixty-four to thirty-two. Numerous senators openly opposed the amendment, some saying that there was no money in the budget to fund such a commission; others felt that the commission, like so many other blue-ribbon commissions, would have no authority to enforce its recommendations."

"Where do things stand at this point?"

"Well, the Senate bill recently passed in that body by a vote of sixty-six to thirty. It easily passed in the House as well, and the President signed it into law today."

"What will happen now?"

"The President has charged the Commissioner of Education with issuing a request for proposals from corporations interested in continuing the computer's development. The Commissioner will review the proposals and recommend an applicant to develop this machine."

"So, things are moving ahead quite rapidly."

"Yes, they are. The Senate has established an Oversight Committee to review the Commissioner's recommendation and appointed Senator Clayton to it. Many Senators expect the committee to act quickly, though, so there will probably be little debate."

Lee liked what Clayton had to say. "I bet the Old Boys in Congress are a little frightened of her." To his mind, this conflict over a super-computer, the development of superhuman technology, is really a conflict between hope and cynicism. Would such a machine save us from ourselves or destroy us? Would money and greed determine the outcome? "Or will we act," he said aloud in sing-song fashion, "with justice and mercy and concern for one another?" The developments of the past few years certainly hadn't encouraged him to think that hope, justice, and concern for one's fellow human beings would win the day.

Lee turned off the motor, lowered the window, and took a deep breath. The air was cold, the tide in. He inhaled deeply again, closed his eyes, and focused on the sound of the ocean. Melted cars, crop circles, suicidal patients, the CIA, Senator Clayton, and Jennings flashed through his mind. He tried to clear it. Another deep breath and a refocus on the sounds of sea and shore: a seagull's call, the surf, a foghorn in the distance. The tensions of the day began to slip into the past.

CHAPTER 6

Winterpool, Maine
Thursday, December 16th, 4:52 P.M.

Americans can always be counted on to do the right
thing when they have exhausted every other option.

~Winston Churchill

L ee started the engine and headed toward home. The radio said
that it might snow again tonight. He pulled the car into the
garage. Still early, it was already pitch dark. Lee hated these winter
evenings when the dark seemed to close in around him from all sides.

He slowly climbed the stairs from the garage to the kitchen. The
blender droned over the audiobook, an Agatha Christie mystery CD.
He didn't know which one. He should. He'd heard all of them. Liz
was busy at the sink. Lee kissed her on the neck, and she turned
with a start.

"How many times do I have to tell you?" she said, with some
irritation. "Don't sneak up on me!"

He smiled and asked absentmindedly how her day had been Not
waiting for her reply, he began to thumb through the day's mail.

"I'll tell you when you're ready to listen," Liz sounded even
more irritated.

"Oh, sorry. Just a lot on my mind today. How was your day?"
Lee asked again, but this time he looked at Liz and waited.

"It was good. Do you want to wait to light the candles? Sharon
always enjoys that; Bill couldn't care less."

"Sure." He was trying to appear interested but wasn't. He'd
even forgotten that they were having old friends over tonight. Bill

and he had worked together and watched years of clinical work take their toll on them both. In recent years, Bill had become a fan of right-wing talk radio. He was a large man but overweight; he no longer exercised. He also drank too much—especially in the last few years—and had high blood pressure to show for it.

Sharon had been a social worker in his office for over thirty years. The last years hadn't been easy for them. But she still tried to support him. The anger that he felt for just about everyone and everything was just beneath the surface and would come out when he drank.

Liz gave him her all-knowing smile. "Okay, get out of here if you're not going to talk or help."

"Hold on, I'll make the salad," said Lee.

"Good. Just park yourself over there, out of my line of travel."

Lee carried the salad makings to the other side of the kitchen. The next few minutes passed without comment. They both found silence reassuring; why, exactly, he didn't know.

The meal was simple: broiled salmon, asparagus, and new potatoes. Mondavi chardonnay for Bill. No hard liquor; they didn't want a repeat of last time. Blueberry pie from the Island Bakery. They hadn't had much time to shop or prepare food, but Bill and Sharon would be fine with that.

"I heard about the fire last night. Did you talk with anyone about it?" asked Liz.

"I had a ring-side seat for it."

"Oh. It had something to do with your client?"

"Not really."

"Some strange things happening around here lately."

"Tell me about it."

The doorbell interrupted their talk. "Well, tell me about it later." Lee nodded. It was 6:30. Right on time, as always.

He and Bill had also been roommates in college. Bill finished his Ph.D. early and interned in Florida. They lost contact for a few years, but, by some stroke of fate, they both ended up in Maine and resumed their friendship. Even with some of his crazy political views, Lee trusted him as a clinician. He'd managed to keep his focus and was respected by his colleagues for his diagnostic work.

Sharon and Liz had met through them and immediately became friends. They shared much in common: they'd both been social workers and had an interest in art and sculpture.

He and Bill had recently had a more difficult time. Old memories provide only so much glue to hold a relationship intact. Lee thought that Bill had become obsessed with money and retirement, and, although he knew it was wrong, he teased Bill about his right-wing viewpoint. He'd asked Bill, on numerous occasions, if he'd fallen down the basement steps, landed on his head, and suffered a right-wing stroke or concussion. So, when the couples had dinner together, conversations were challenging sometimes, and tonight would likely be no different.

Sharon and Liz lit the Sabbath candles and sang the Jewish prayers. "*Baruch ata Adonai, Eloheynu Melech ha'olam. Asher kidshanu be'mitzvotav ve'tzivanu le'hadlik ner shel Shabbath.*"

Lee followed. "Holy one of blessing your presence fills creation commanding us to light the Sabbath lights."

The evening began with lighter topics. The Patriots were still in the playoffs, maybe the Super Bowl. The Congregational Church had finally gotten its heating system repaired. And there were a number of sightings last night of strange lights in the sky. This led, of course, to a discussion of the fire and of the melted car that was being talked about around town. Lee was quiet. Bill decided to change the subject.

"So, Lee, what do you think about Clayton?" asked Bill mischievously. "Where the hell did she come from?"

"I don't know," said Lee, trying to avoid the subject. "What do you think?"

Bill leaned back from the table. "I think she has no experience. She's only been a senator for four years, and she's from LA. California is as much like the rest of this country as Mars."

Bill, unfortunately, was on his third glass of wine and was starting to sound like it.

"She wants to put more restrictions and regulations on IT development. She sounds anti-tech to me. That won't get her very far. We can't go back, can we?"

Lee turned to Liz to offer her more wine, which he knew she would refuse, and rolled his eyes. An awkward silence ensued.

"Some days I wish we could," Lee muttered. Then he spoke up, "We certainly don't know how to control the technology we have. Look at how many people are controlled by their technology. Slaves to the Internet. And our children, constantly on gadgets. Some days it seems like no one talks to anyone directly. Making eye contact and *saying* words have become things of the past. If they can't text someone, our kids don't know how to talk to them." Lee's face was getting redder as he talked. Bill had touched a nerve.

Liz joined the conversation to calm things down, Lee thought. But he was wrong. The Singularity was an issue for her, too.

"So, Bill," asked Liz, "what are we, the creators of computers, going to do when they become smarter than we are and begin designing machines that become smarter than all humanity combined? Will we still be in control? I don't think so. This is something that needs to be dealt with, like global warming, while there's still time."

Lee jumped back in, thinking that he would try to end the discussion on a positive note. "I think that Clayton is a new voice, Bill. She's talking about hope, and I think we all need that right now. The fear that has controlled politics in this country for the last twenty-five years hasn't gotten us anyplace. Maybe she *is* a bit anti-tech, but don't we need to be having that debate?" He shrugged. "Although I'm sure that could affect the bottom line for the IT companies, God forbid."

Sharon hadn't said anything, and Bill had fallen silent from the double- teaming of Lee and Liz. But Lee could sense that Bill was nearly back on his feet and ready to fight. And, as Lee expected, he knew just what to say.

"And she's a woman. And we all know what happened to the last one of those who ran for president."

Lee inhaled deeply; he knew that Liz couldn't pass on that one.

"What does being a woman have to do with anything?" she snapped.

"I just don't like it," said Bill. "I'm not sure what she would do if we were attacked again. I'd just feel more comfortable with a man being at the controls. Even Sharon agrees with me on this one." Bill looked at Sharon.

Oh, God, not tonight, thought Lee.

"Do you?" asked Liz, glaring at Sharon.

Sharon looked down at her plate. "Well . . . well, ah, I don't know," Sharon said in a whisper. She looked at Bill. "I mean," she said, with no conviction, "what would a woman — what would she do if there was a major war?"

Liz turned again to Bill and rolled her eyes. "Well, maybe she'd be less likely to drag us into a major war."

"That's what I mean." Bill said. "Under-reaction could get us killed."

"Well, overreaction has certainly gotten a lot of young men and women killed over the last few years," Liz snapped.

And so it went until Lee suggested that he make coffee and they served dessert. The break allowed them to calm down a bit, and, afterward, Lee took Bill aside. "I need a little case consultation, my friend."

"Okay."

Bill seemed a bit surprised but made an effort to look and sound professional. The wine was starting to wear off a bit, Lee thought.

"What's up?"

"Dreams," said Lee, "the same ones, night after night." "Not unusual," responded Bill.

"Something is different about these." Lee gave a brief review of the dreams that Frank had reported. "They make no sense to him. He says they don't relate to him or to any of the issues I've worked on with him."

Bill nodded. "Strong affect associated with the dreams?"

"No. So far, he seems relatively disinterested in them. Sort of like infomercials on a radio or television monitor or Facebook." Lee shrugged. "He shows about that much interest in them."

"Resistant to talk about them?"

"No, not at all," said Lee.

"Do they relate to anything happening in his life now?"

"I don't think so. At least neither of us has been able to make any connections. The dreams remind me of those that Dr.—I can't recall his name—wrote about; you know, that kooky guy who wrote about alien abductions? Remember? I think it was in the late eighties. He sent copies to most of the psychologists in New England. Whatever happened to him?"

"I don't know," said Bill, sounding less interested. He began rubbing his neck. "Damn wine. My neck stiffens up every time I drink."

Lee had considered telling Bill about his own dream of the *Carol Deering*. But he didn't. He'd deal with that when he got back, before he saw Frank again—*if* he saw Frank again. He realized that Bill had drunk too much to provide anything more in the way of useful assistance.

Sharon interrupted their conversation, looking at her watch. "It's time to go, honey. We should give Liz the rest of the night to pack." She knew Liz too well.

They said their goodbyes and wished Lee and Liz good travel and a great, albeit short, vacation.

After they left, Lee cleaned up and put the dishes away. Liz went upstairs, indeed, to continue packing. In the past, a conversation like this would have Lee on edge, but this one didn't. He understood his friend's extreme conservatism, especially in the past few years, as having its roots in his past, with his efforts to make a place for himself in a world that often viewed him and his "race" with contempt. Liz and Bill were both Jews and first-generation Americans who'd taken very different paths in dealing with the anti-Semitism they'd faced throughout their lives.

Tonight, Lee went to bed before Liz. His mind drifted to his client, who apparently was okay but hadn't reappeared, and his visit from Jennings. Were they connected? Lee just knew it, even though Jennings had been quick to deny it. He didn't trust Jennings; he'd learned not to. Jennings had lied to him before, all in the service of our country Lee was sure. What was really going on? Did Jennings know more about all of this than he was saying? He must. And that guy, Andy, CIA, and an important package to be picked up and delivered. Lee kept rolling all of this over in his brain until he finally fell asleep.

CHAPTER 7

Office of Dick Chambers, CEO, Hollocore
Dallas, Texas
Friday, December 17th, 1:45 P.M. CST

Without regard for the wishes of men, any machines
or techniques or forms of organization that can
economically replace men do replace men.

~ **KURT VONNEGUT,**
Player Piano

Dick Chambers sat behind a large mahogany desk. A small man in his late sixties, he had numerous health problems, mainly cardiac, although some would question whether or not he had a heart. He was known as a ruthless businessman and an archconservative.

A picture of his two daughters lived on his desk, although he hadn't seen one of them in over twenty years. He also had a picture of his wife, who lived in Washington, DC. She chose to stay there when Chambers returned to Texas to run Hollocore. With his schedule, he only saw her once or twice a month. They talked occasionally on the phone.

His was a corner office on the top floor of a building built by Hollocore. The chairs were large, with heavy wood and leather. The walls were covered with photographs and plaques, many from the years that Chambers had served in Congress. He especially treasured the one of himself and Ronald Reagan.

Chambers got up and walked toward the bank of windows looking out on the Dallas skyline. It was a cloudy, gray day, not unusual for Dallas in December. He was waiting for someone who was late. Dick Chambers did not like tardiness. He fidgeted with the good-luck piece in his pocket, a coin commemorating Dallas's 100th anniversary.

He looked again at his watch, a Rolex that he also treasured, mainly because he felt good about how much he'd paid: fifty percent below retail. The intercom buzzed.

"Yes, Cynthia."

"Mr. Collins is here to see you, sir."

"Show him in."

The heavy wood door to his office opened to admit a large man wearing a custom-made suit and Italian shoes—wo items that Chambers considered a waste of money.

Chambers' guest offered no apology for his tardiness. He extended his hand, a gesture that Chambers ignored.

"How are you, Dick?" asked Collins.

"Well, you tell me, Robert. That's what I'm paying you for."

Robert Collins took a seat in front of Chambers' desk. Chambers remained standing but removed his QuickPad from the corner of the desk. Collins was a lobbyist, a very good and very highly paid one.

"I assume you're referring to the upcoming vote on your contract that the Senate Oversight Committee will be reviewing."

Chambers nodded impatiently. Collins was one of the few people who wasn't afraid of him, and Chambers knew it.

"Well, we've got the votes. Clayton and Greenwood won't be able to derail this, so you guys can start spending the money."

"You're sure of this?" He looked Collins straight in the eye.

"We've got the votes. Dick, I told you your company's money would be well spent."

"I know you didn't fly all the way down here just to tell me that."

He chuckled. "Of course not. I have business down here with some of your friends and possible competitors."

The conversation paused.

"So, can you do it?" asked Collins, "build a computer smarter than the entire human race?"

Chambers didn't respond at first. Collins waited.

Chambers finally looked up from his QPad. "Well, given that the computer only has to be smarter than humans, I'm sure we're up to it."

Collins smiled and chuckled again. Chambers stepped toward the door, but Collins didn't move.

"Mr. Collins, I have a board meeting in five minutes. Please be on time for our next meeting, assuming that we will have one."

Collins smiled again. "Oh, I'm sure there'll be one." Collins rose and moved toward the door, exiting with "Happy Holidays, Dick."

Chambers didn't respond. He let the door close behind Collins and walked to another leading from his office into the boardroom. He paused for a few seconds then cracked the door. Board members were taking their seats around a huge mahogany table for which Chambers himself supervised the construction. When he entered, the Board members stood and waited. He sat down and motioned for the others to do so.

"This will be a brief meeting, and off the record," he announced to the board's recording secretary, who nodded agreement. "Hollocore is poised to take the next giant step in IT." Chambers looked down at his hands folded on the table. "The Europeans once again are asking for the United States to bail them out." He smirked. "They're not capable of finishing the supercomputer project they began." He paused then looked up. "So, what's new?" He chuckled, as did everyone else.

"They're happy to give the product they've created to our government, which has accepted it. The Commissioner of Education will issue a request for proposals to finish the project, to which we, as you know, and three other companies will respond." Chambers scanned the room. "Two of these companies will not be chosen, because they lack the capability, the human brain power, to complete the project. "Our only real competitor is TransSea. But Robert

Collins, our lobbyist, has assured me that the recommendation of the Commissioner will be positive for us and will be accepted by the Senate subcommittee that reviews the project. He anticipates that no one on the committee will be able to block us, although I'm sure that some would do so if they could."

Chambers perused the room again. All eight board members were present. All men; all chosen by Chambers. Hollocore had never had a female board member. They were now smiling and nodding in agreement. Chambers waited. The Vice Chair began to applaud and the others followed.

"However, there is one issue. I believe it a minor one. Because of the problems in the past two weeks with electronic data transfers and the sensitive nature of the project, the United States government will assign a courier to pick up the EU's product in Paris and deliver it to Boston." He paused. "I have instructed our Director of Security, Reginald Brown," he looked directly at Mr. Brown, who smiled nervously, "to take all steps necessary to see that the courier and the package arrive safely in Boston. Mr. Brown has assured me that he and his staff will make it so." He again looked at Mr. Brown, as did the other board members. "I will keep the board informed of developments as needed." With that, he adjourned the meeting and returned to his office.

Dick Chambers should have been pleased with himself. Hollocore would get the contract. Collins had assured him of that. But he wasn't pleased. Had he missed an opportunity for himself and Hollocore? He'd seen another article this morning in the *Financial Times* on TransSea's plans to send a mining probe to Beta 17 as it passed Earth next month. "It should be a Hollocore probe," he grumbled. But Chambers had listened to his scientists rather than his own intuition. They'd said that it was too risky.

Mining minerals on an asteroid? Still the stuff of science fiction, they'd said. Chambers had listened to them, and now he regretted it.

CHAPTER 8

Lee's Home
Winterpool, Maine
Friday, December 17th, 8:15 A.M.

Be kind, for everyone you meet is fighting a hard battle.

~ Plato

Lee didn't sleep well and woke early. He sat on the edge of the bed and stared out at the ocean. What to tell Liz? Maybe Jennings and "Howdy Doody" would find another delivery boy. Maybe he could avoid them in London. They hadn't asked him to do anything yet. Maybe they wouldn't. Lee could wait to tell her. There. He'd talked himself out of saying anything to Liz, something he'd done many times before. But this time, he caught himself. He knew that wasn't the best way to handle things with Liz. It'd be hard. She'd ask a dozen questions, as always. But he'd tell her about what had happened. What might happen.

They had breakfast together at least once a week, at the same diner they'd been going to for years. The place was busy, as usual. The diner walls were lined with toys that Gail collected with a passion, starting in November, for the Marines. "Toys for Tots." Louie, who had opened the diner with his wife Gail after he'd gotten back from Vietnam, was at the grill. The two were a strange combination. He was tall and thin; Gail was barely five feet. She was always smiling and talking; Louie seldom said a word to anyone outside of the kitchen.

Lee and Liz took the last table, which was near the front door. Liz was debating whether to sit at the counter because of the draft. Lee sat down. Liz stood for a few seconds but soon gave up and joined him.

The waitress came. Julie. "The usual?" she asked. "Coffee, two eggs over easy for you," she said, looking at Lee, "with bacon and raisin toast. And, for you, tea, two poached eggs with rye toast, hold the butter. Right?" Lee nodded and smiled.

"Remember," said Liz, "hold the butter."

Liz made a few comments about the packing she still had to do. Lee smiled and nodded but said nothing.

"Lee, what are you thinking about?" Lee still didn't respond. "Lee, we're on vacation," said Liz, trying to get him to look in her direction.

"You've been looking forward to this. What's going on?"

He continued to avoid her eyes. "Oh, honey, I'm fine. Fine. I just have a few things on my mind."

"Well, that's obvious. You kept mumbling in your sleep last night. I couldn't make out what you were saying."

"Yeah, yeah, I know. Just a little confused and worried I guess." Liz continued to stare.

"Jennings showed up in my office yesterday." He looked away and waited, but not for long.

"Jennings? Oh, no!" Liz exploded, and Lee grimaced. "What did *he* want? I thought we were done with him. Aren't we?"

Lee noticed that the couple sitting at the table closest to them had turned to listen to the conversation.

"Liz, please, I'm not sure that the other people here are really interested." Although they obviously were.

Liz waited.

"Well, I thought so, but he said he might need me to do a small favor."

"Small favor?" retorted Liz, raising her voice again. "Those guys don't deserve any favors. Large or small. They owe you, our daughter, and me!"

Lee felt his neck and face getting quite warm and assumed that they were growing redder by the second. He made another effort to calm Liz.

He leaned in, lowering his voice. "I know, I know, Liz. But they still have the upper hand." He paused. "And I have no doubt they would use it."

Liz, finally aware of the risk of being overheard, followed Lee's cue. "So, what's this small favor?" Her voice was just a step above a hush.

"He wants me to pick up something in London and deliver it to someone in Paris."

"Great," Liz said, rolling her eyes. "The first time we've been out of the States, just you and me, since I don't know when, and he wants you to play Federal Express?"

"Look, I don't like this any better than you do, but we'll just have to see what happens. They'll contact me in London if they still..."

Liz interrupted. "Can Joe..."

Lee cut her off. "No, no. We don't need to get poor Joe involved in this again." Joe was Lee's attorney and close friend. "We've created enough of a problem for him. Last time, they almost got him disbarred."

Lee took Liz's hand. "Look at me." He paused until she looked up. "Let's just see what happens." As if on cue, their meals arrived, and the routine of their life continued for now.

The day passed quickly. Final packing, a call to Dru, a somewhat compulsive round of checking the house to see what was turned off, turned down, and/or locked before leaving. Lee checked the front door three times.

The drive to Portland, the flight to Boston, and check-in and security in Boston went smoothly. It was a beautiful day.

The plane to London was packed. Thank God, they weren't in the middle. Lee took the window seat. Liz liked being on the aisle. She could snag whoever was occupying the other aisle seat or might stroll by for a chat. Today's guest in 7C was Ms. Politically Correct 2027, a soccer mom—Lee thought they were still called that—from the Cape, who, after polite introductions, launched into a discussion on private versus public education. Lee groaned, politely smiled, and dove into his QPad at the first opportunity. Liz joined the debate.

Dru had gone to a private school for her high school years. Lee had always had mixed feelings about that — well, not that mixed; they were mostly negative. Lee and Liz, the great advocates for public education, had given in to their daughter. The transition back to Maine was sudden and not of Dru's choosing. Lee had moved the family back to Tennessee when Dru was three. But after ten years of fundamentalism and right-wing politics, they were ready to return to Maine. Lee went back to his Maine practice, and Liz retired from social work and went to art school, something she'd always wanted to do.

They'd put Dru in a small private school, thinking that it would help with the transition. They were right. After the first year, she loved it and wanted to stay. The school was a bastion of liberalism, and, after having lived in the South for many years, Lee had to admit that it was refreshing, at least at first. But he also felt that it was a bastion of some hypocrisy. During a fundraiser that the school had sponsored for some poor Indian tribe in South America, the discussion had turned to ways of raising additional money for the cause. Lee's suggestion of taking the children out of private school for a year and putting the tuition they saved into the cause had not been, to say the least, well received. This was a group that definitely did not know how to take a joke.

Late afternoon became early evening. The sky was dark, but the air smooth. As the hours passed, conversations faded. Liz closed her book, one of those English mysteries she loved, and put on her eyeshades. The woman across the aisle also settled in for the night.

Lee couldn't sleep. He seldom could on airplanes. The World Health Organization materials from the workshop he was to attend in Paris weren't holding his attention. For Lee, long flights, just like long showers, were good times to think. They were time markers.

Their last flight to Europe had been with Dru, a trip to Paris for her sixteenth birthday. She'd loved it, and so had Lee and Liz. Since then, the years had seemed to fly by. He'd already had a long life—considerably longer one than some of his childhood friends who'd died at the ripe old age of nineteen in Vietnam. He had much to be grateful for. As part of his personal campaign to practice gratitude, which he'd decided to undertake while in detention in Boston, he'd become involved in public education activities that involved leading discussions about the change process.

Without question, the country needed a good dose of resilience, but bouncing back from the last few years had been, to say the least, a challenge. Coupled with racism, the failure to change things enough and as quickly as his base expected had almost done in the previous president. And America's unrealistic and divisive wish list was in the process of taking the present one down. But from talks with his community, Lee had begun to believe that maybe people were getting more realistic in seeing what they had, what they should be grateful for, and what needed to change. People were seeing that they could control only themselves and change their world only by changing themselves.

It also seemed to Lee that people were again exhibiting one of America's core values: caring for one's neighbors. At least he hoped so. The new voice on the political stage, Senator Clayton, had a message different from other politicians. Her words sounded to Lee a lot like those of Jack Kennedy, asking, as Kennedy had, "not what your country can do for you, ask what you can do for your country," Senator Clayton would say, "It is not all about you; it's about us."

Lee was finally starting to feel drowsy. He thought of another flight with Dru when she was sixteen—that is, sixteen months. They'd flown to Toronto to visit Liz's family. Dru had slept most of the way on his lap. Lee pulled the blanket up to his chin and crossed his arms, remembering how warm she'd felt lying on his chest.

When he woke, the sky was lighter. People were starting to stir.

They would be landing at Heathrow soon, around 9:00 A.M. London time.

CHAPTER 9

Heathrow
London, England
Saturday, December 18th, 9:16 A.M.

Heathrow was busy, as always, perhaps a bit more so because it was a Saturday morning. And their luggage actually arrived with the flight. Given the frequent meltdowns that the airport had with its luggage systems, Lee was surprised. Lee's bag, "the thing," as Liz called it, was always easy to find on the belt. It was bright red and bigger than most. Liz complained that Lee packed for a month when he was only going for a week.

The attendant was missing from the taxi stand. Lee saw a free taxi and headed for it, pulling "the thing" behind him. He didn't see the car; he just heard Liz shout, "Lee, look out!"

He glanced to his left and instinctively jumped back, landing on the suitcase. A nondescript black sedan whipped past, narrowly missing him. The driver from the taxi that Lee was trying to reach yelled, "Bloody fool," and offered Lee a hand up. Liz was at his side.

"Are you all right?"

"I'm okay. I'm fine," grumbled Lee, dusting himself off.

The driver loaded their luggage into the back of the taxi, still muttering, "Bloody fool." Lee wasn't sure whether he was referring to him or the driver of the sedan. He didn't ask.

The Thistle Marble Arch was, of course, near the Marble Arch at Hyde Park. They'd stayed there years before. It was an older hotel with a lot of wood and overstuffed furniture. The small lobby had an adjoining bar and restaurant that reminded Lee of the Parker House in Boston.

"Sir, do you require assistance with your luggage?" asked the clerk.

Lee wasn't listening. He was still thinking about the airport. The driver hadn't sounded his horn or stopped. He'd quickly disappeared into traffic.

Sir?"

"No, no. We can handle it," replied Lee, shaking his head.

"Where are you, Lee?" asked Liz.

"I'm here, right here," he replied, raising his voice and giving her one of those don't-ask-any-more-questions looks.

But Liz, not to be deterred, responded, "No, you aren't. You're thinking about something."

Liz always could read his face. Lee pushed the elevator button. It was stuck. He pushed it again then banged on it. The light finally came on.

"Did you see who was driving the car at the airport?" The elevator door rattled open. It was empty. They stepped in, and Lee pushed six.

"No, I didn't. The windows were dark, like those of a limousine."

"Privacy glass all around," said Lee.

"I assume so. What are you thinking?" But Liz answered her own question: "You're thinking that it wasn't an accident, right? And it's got something to do with Jennings and the package you may have to pick up."

Lee hesitated. "Well, I don't know." He shook his head. "No, I'm sure it was just me. My peripheral vision isn't very good anymore."

The elevator door opened hesitantly on the sixth floor. Room 625 was halfway down a long hall. Lee tried to herd Liz down the hall quickly.

"Stop pushing," she objected. "What's the rush?"

He gave up and walked at her pace. He opened the door. The room was small, but had all the basics: two beds, a television, a vanity, a desk, and a couple of chairs. Lee double-locked the door and checked to make sure that the windows were locked.

"Do you mind, Mr. Paranoia, if I take a shower, or do you want to check the bathroom first?" asked Liz with a smirk.

"Very funny. I'm fine. I'll just start unpacking." With some effort, he threw his bag onto the bed nearest to the door.

"She's right. The damn thing is heavy," he mumbled, unzipping the bag. "Maybe I just wasn't looking."

Lee pulled out the black silk suit he loved and started shaking and beating the wrinkles out. Sometimes that worked; other times it looked like he'd backed a car over it.

Liz had just turned the shower on when the phone rang. Lee picked up the receiver, but before he could speak, the caller did.

"Dr. Brazil?"

"Yes, this is Dr. Brazil."

"Mr. Smith requests that you go to The Fusilier Museum, Her Majesty's Tower of London, at three thirty tomorrow afternoon. Do not be early or late. You will receive instruction from the museum's ticket agent as to the package's location."

"Can you tell me . . ." But the line went dead.

Lee returned to unpacking. "That wasn't Smith or Jennings; I'd have recognized their voices. The caller had a British accent," Lee mumbled. "Brilliant. Most of the population has a British accent. You're in London, dummy." Lee laughed at himself. "This whole thing has really got me rattled." When Liz emerged, he was lying on the bed and thumbing through a guide to London restaurants, still talking to himself.

"So, what are we doing for dinner?" asked Liz.

"Indian, I think. I'm not sure that I have a real urge for kidney pie or steak and potatoes. Indian is always the safer bet in London."

"Great. I'm hungry. It's been hours since we ate."

Lee objected, "Come on, honey, it's too early. My body says we should still be in bed." He yawned. "It's only 6:00 A.M. back home."

"It's almost noon here," she countered. "How about room service?" "Sure. Do what you like." He was losing interest in the conversation.

Liz ordered a steak sandwich and chips, but Lee's stomach wasn't ready for anything more than coffee. He was still thinking about the airport.

After lunch, they took a nap—at least they tried to. Lee knew that it was against all advice about jet lag, but he closed his eyes, assuming that he wouldn't drift into sleep, but he did. He dreamed. He was in a Coast Guard station. The sign read Jacksonville Beach Station. Through a door marked Radio Room, he could hear a distress call that was coming in. He opened the door and stepped inside. The radio operator was busy responding to the call and didn't notice Lee. A man's voice broke through the static. "This is *The Enchantress*. We are in trouble. We are off the coast of Charleston. Our position is . . ." Static distorted the rest of the message.

"Repeat," said the Guardsman.

The man complied, but the message was still garbled.

The Guardsman requested that *The Enchantress* start a long count so that he could ascertain the exact position of the ship. The man's voice started the count: "One, two, three, four . . ." In a minute, the count was taken up by a child's voice: "Eight-four, eight-five, eight-six, eighty-seven." The tones got weaker and weaker until the child's voice faded out completely.

"*Enchantress*, we have dispatched Search and Rescue. Hang on. We're coming. Please continue the count." But the only sound from the radio was static. Lee woke up.

"What the hell is happening to me?" he mumbled. He'd found an old newspaper article in the *Winterpool Gazette*'s archives the week before. *The Enchantress* had disappeared off the coast of Charleston in 1963. The Coast Guard's Search and Rescue squad, which had been immediately dispatched along with Navy vessels, found no sign of the fifty-nine-foot yacht or the three adults and the two children who were aboard.

My God, I'm having the same kind of dreams as my patient. I'm losing distance. I have to get out of this business. He tried to go back to sleep but couldn't. When he started to drift off, the distress call would just replay.

He finally got up and decided to wander down to the concierge. He needed a distraction. He engaged the concierge in a conversation about new restaurants in London. At the man's recommendation, Lee booked a six o'clock reservation at the Cinnamon Club in Westminster, which, according to the man, offered "a constantly evolving menu designed to reflect an ethos of innovation and creativity." Traditional Indian food would have been fine with Lee, but why not try something new? The concierge insisted that it was the place to go.

When Lee returned to the room, Liz was just waking up.

"Want to take a walk?" he asked. "We can get some exercise and fresh air before we head for the restaurant. Maybe see a bit of the park, and then we can catch a taxi or the tube."

"Boy, you're full of energy," said Liz, trying to find her reading glasses, which apparently had fallen off the nightstand. Lee waited. "But a good idea," said Liz. "I think that might take my headache away."

It was sunny and warm, at least by Maine standards, in the low fifties. Rare weather for late December in London.

They entered Hyde Park through the Marble Arch and walked toward the Italian gardens. Lee noted that a man in a long, brown trench coat had been a few yards behind them since they'd left the hotel. Maybe he's just out for a few rays of winter sun, Lee thought, but when they turned toward Paddington Station to catch the Underground to Kensington Station, he was still behind them.

The station was crowded with families who'd taken in the unusually good weather and were returning home. Lee pulled Liz through the crowd toward the train.

"What's your hurry, Lee?"

"I don't want to be late," he said with a nervous smile.

"Relax, we're early. And I want to look at those handbags

over there," said Liz, pointing to a small shop on the other side of the station.

Lee gave her another tug. "You can look when we get to Kensington.

They'll have shops there."

She resisted. "I'm not sure they'll have that bag."

Lee caught her eye. "Liz, come on. Now!"

She finally realized that something was happening and followed Lee. The platform for their train was jammed. Lee pressed into the crowd, hoping that it might swallow them, but the man was still there, just a few feet away, waiting for the same train.

When the train arrived, Lee shoved their way into the car. They passed a number of empty seats and moved to the opposite end of the car.

"Hey, here are two seats." Liz started to sit down.

Lee yanked her out of the seat. "No, I want to sit by the door."

"Jesum crow, Lee, take it easy with my arm. What is wrong with you?"

Lee didn't respond. He was watching the man in the trench coat, who boarded the train and took a seat in the middle of the car. Just as Liz was about to sit down again, Lee gave her another yank. "Changed my mind," he said and pushed her through the closing car doors and onto the platform. The man moved toward the doors but too late.

"What was that all about?" Liz sounded disgusted. "You've been dragging me around like that old leather briefcase of yours!"

Lee sighed. "I'm sorry, honey. But some guy was following us. I don't like being followed."

"Well, we can catch the next one."

"No, I think we should stay near the hotel. Remember the Mahal? It's just around the corner, on Edgware." They'd gone there on their last visit. They, Dru included, had loved the food and the place. It was one of the oldest Indian restaurants in London. *Avant-garde* it wasn't, but it *was* relaxed and friendly, just what they needed right now.

The restaurant wasn't crowded, and the waiter showed them to a small table by a window.

"Who do you think would have us followed, Lee? I thought in this new age of technology, they'd watch us with a satellite microchip." Liz paused. "Unless the guy in the trench coat was supposed to do something that a satellite couldn't do."

"Like what?" asked Lee.

"Like keep you from picking up the package."

"I have no idea, but I'm sure that it does have something to do with the damn package I'm supposed to pick up tomorrow."

"Tomorrow? How do you know that it's tomorrow? How do you know you're supposed to pick the package up anyway?"

Lee avoided her stare. "Someone called while you were in the shower." "Oh, Lee. I have a bad feeling about this. It's all starting again."

Lee rubbed the tip of his hook against the palm of his hand. "Maybe I'm wrong. Maybe I'm just letting my imagination get away with me. But why would the man . . ." He stopped. "Good grief, it does sound like a spy novel! But why would he try to get off the train when we did?"

Liz shook her head with conviction. "Oh, no, I don't think it's your imagination. But what can we do?"

"Follow instructions, I guess." He looked at her. "Unless you have a better idea?"

"No," said Liz softly.

Lee stared out the window. It was dark. Only a few people walked along the street. When he spoke, his voice was soft and deep.

"After that year in Boston, I guess I'm surprised that they even let me on the plane." He didn't look at Liz. "We don't need any more trouble."

As they ate, they talked some about Dru and her boyfriend and how serious things seemed to be getting. They talked about Val, the friend that Liz was meeting in London for the shopping trip.

Liz finally asked about the elephant in the room. "So, tomorrow?"

"Three-thirty sharp. 'Don't be early, don't be late,'" said Lee with a cadence. "The Tower of London. The Fusilier Museum. These folks do have a sense of humor."

"I'm not laughing," said Liz, as she finished the last bit of goat's milk ice cream.

Their walk back to the hotel was brisk, given the dark and the way the temperature had dropped. The winter cold in London always seemed to get through even the heaviest of clothing. Lee recalled that, for some reason, most of his visits to London had been in winter.

He kept looking back, but no one was on the streets now. The hotel lobby was also deserted, but for one man at the bar: A large man, dark skin, well-dressed. He looked in their direction as they boarded the elevator.

The room was cold, so Liz turned up the heat, and they both began preparing for bed. Lee wasn't sure that they could sleep, but this was what they always did this time of the evening.

Liz broke the silence. "When are we going to talk about this more?"

"I don't know what else to say. Sleep late. Have brunch here, and I'll go over to the Tower early. I've never seen it; maybe I'll take the tour."

"Lee, if you're going to act like a tourist, I'm going."

"Well, damn it, Liz, that's what we are . . . and you're *not* going."

"I'm going," she said, giving him her don't-waste-your-time-arguing-with-me look.

He sighed. "Okay, okay. Let's just get this over. I'll pick up the friggin' package, drop it off, and be done with this whole thing. At least I hope I'm done. I didn't realize that this business with Jennings would be a life sentence."

Liz put her hand out. Lee took it. They turned off the lights and tried to sleep. In a few minutes, Lee was up, checking the door.

Double-bolted but no chain. He rolled his suitcase over and wedged it between the door and the bureau. Someone would wake the dead getting through the door now.

Lee drifted in and out of sleep. He dreamed of the man in the brown trench coat. Lee was pulling Liz through the crowd at Paddington Station, the man in the coat in close pursuit, reaching for Liz. When Lee awoke, he realized that he'd pulled Liz onto his side of the bed.

"What is it?" Alarmed, Liz pulled herself away and fumbled for the canister of pepper spray she'd placed on the nightstand.

"Nothing. Just a dream. It's okay. It's okay."

"What?" Liz asked again.

Lee reached out and touched her shoulder. "Go back to sleep."

In the morning, The Thing was still wedged between the bureau and the door. No one had tried to enter.

CHAPTER 10

Office of Police Chief Moore
Winterpool, Maine
Saturday, December 18th, 11:15 A.M.

C hief Moore was on the phone with Dorothy Crosby, a member of the Town Council. "Yes, Dorothy. I know, Dorothy. I'm just as concerned as you are with the safety of our children." He rolled his eyes. "Yes, yes, I agree, but I don't think that putting armed guards in each of our schools is the answer." The intercom buzzed.

"Hold on, Dorothy."

"Yes, Abby." "Frank Bowman."

"Oh, yes. Tell him to come in."

"Dorothy, I'll have to call you back." Chief Moore hung up and grumbled, "I suppose the next thing they're going to want to do is put bars over school windows."

Abby opened the door, and Frank stepped in sheepishly.

The Chief stepped forward. "Come in, Frank. We've been worried about you. Dr. Brazil was sure something had happened to you." Frank nodded but didn't speak, as he took a chair.

"You're lucky. The propane tanks of that cabin you rented for the winter leaked. If you and Doc had been inside, the Fire Marshal says you both would've been incinerated. So, where've you been?"

Frank finally spoke, "Chief, I don't know exactly what happened that night. I loaded my stuff into the back of my car. I was moving out. I wasn't going to put my wife through any more. But as I got closer to the cabin . . ." He shuffled his feet. "I had . . . I got this strange feeling that I shouldn't stop, that I should just kept on driving. So, I did. I drove for hours. Ended up somewhere in upstate New York." He looked away. "Called my wife the next day; we talked, and I came home. I think we're doing okay." He looked at the Chief again. "And those dreams that had scared the hell out of me, the ones I went to Doc for, have gone." He snapped his fingers. "Just like that."

Frank stood and shook hands with Chief Moore. "I just wanted to say how sorry I am for the trouble I caused you and your officers."

"Okay," said the Chief. "Just . . . just take care of yourself and your family."

Frank closed the door, and the Chief leaned against his desk, arms crossed. "Sounds pretty strange to me, and still doesn't explain those weird circles. Can't figure that one out. Oh, well." He sat down at his desk and began going through the last shift report.

Now in his late fifties, Moore looked younger than his years, even with white hair. He'd been dealing with people and situations he didn't understand for most of his career. He'd given up trying to find all the answers years ago. That was one way that he maintained his sanity.

Just after college, his first job had been as a part-time police officer in South Beach. He needed the money and was unsure what to do with himself. By summer's end, he was hooked. Under some stroke of luck, South Beach was looking for a full-time officer. He took the job. The money wasn't great, and he was one of only a few cops with a college degree, a fact that a couple of officers never let him forget.

Ambitious, moved steadily through the ranks. He met a young woman and married. She worked. They both worked. They had to; he wasn't able to support a family on just his salary. He passed the sergeant's exam, and life became better for the youngest sergeant in a department of three.

But police work began to change him. He became more cynical, more suspicious. He and his wife fought more, and he drank more. He found that alcohol could swallow up sad or angry feelings very quickly, at least for a few hours. But he didn't like what was happening.

One Friday afternoon, he was working alone and responded

to a call, a bad accident on Route 1. On arrival, he thought that he recognized the car, that it belonged to his sister, who was babysitting his five-year-old. The car had overturned after hitting a tree, scattering children's clothing all over the ground. He could do little for the young woman and her child. It wasn't his sister and his son, but, after working the accident, after the ambulance and the tow truck had gone and the crowd had left, he drove to his sister's house. His son was surprised and happy to see him. He hugged the boy and decided to change his life.

And he did. He didn't, couldn't, given up police work; he loved it. But he developed interests and friendships outside of the department. He decided not to be like other cops and just hang out with cops. He also found some help. He saw a counselor and learned to talk about what was going on with him.

He'd taken the job with Winterpool twenty years ago. He still talked about that Friday afternoon that had changed his life. He emphasized to new recruits that taking care of themselves and their families is key. Chief Moore considered himself a success. He loved his job. He wasn't an alcoholic. He was still married to the woman he'd fallen in love with thirty years ago. He had a good relationship with his children.

No, he didn't make a lot of money being the police chief of a small Maine town, but, as he would say, God knows that a lot of things are worth a lot more than money.

CHAPTER 11

The Saint
Boston Harbor, Boston, Massachusetts
Saturday, December 18th, 1:35 P.M.

Joann got through customs without any trouble. She checked her bag and was told to proceed to the boarding entrance for staff on the second level. As she approached the entrance, she had a feeling that she was being watched. She was. A young woman in a ship officer's pressed and spotless white uniform was watching her approach.

"I am Ellen Zan." She had short blond hair and bright green eyes—a bit mannish and robotic for Joann's taste, but a handsome woman nonetheless. "Welcome aboard *The Saint,* Joann Lawrence. I will show you to your quarters and take you to the children. Please follow me."

Joann was impressed by both Ellen Zan and the quarters: a comfortable stateroom on the outside of the ship, with a porthole and double bed. "I am sure that you will be comfortable here."

Joann nodded. "Yes, I'm sure."

"I have much to do, so I will take you to the children now. They are in the Children's Game Room," said Zan, walking briskly down the corridor. Joann had to pick up her pace to keep up.

Zan opened the door of a large room filled with an assortment of electronic games, but the children were sitting at a table with another crew member playing a card game, Old Maid.

Zan addressed the man. "You may go now, Richard. I will take over."

The crewman complied, and she introduced Joann. "Children, this is the woman who will be taking care of you for the next few days:

Miss Lawrence." She turned to Joann. "Please meet Thomas and John Belton. Their mother will be down shortly. I will see you later."

Just like that, Zan took her leave and left Joann with the children. Thomas looked about six and John about nine. They extended their hands. Joann knelt so that they were face to face.

"Glad to meet you," she said, as she shook their hands. "I haven't played Old Maid in a very long time. Is that one of your favorite games?"

They both nodded. Thomas was dressed in shorts and John in what looked like knickers, even though it was late December in Boston. John was also wearing something that Joann hadn't seen for a long time: a Madras shirt. Both boys were blond, blue eyed, and in need of a haircut.

They finished the Old Maid game. Tommy won. Mrs. Belton hadn't appeared, so Joann opened the bag that she'd brought with her.

"Guys, why don't we try to find some new games on the Internet?" Both children stared at her blankly, as she pulled out her QPad.

Thomas spoke up first. "What's that? A little television?" "Oh, you haven't seen one of these yet?" Both boys shook their heads.

"Let's go to NPR and see if we can find some *Sesame Street* games."

Thomas looked at John. "What's *Sesame Street*?"

"You know, Tommy. Remember, Mom told us about it? It's one of those new things that we're learning about."

"Oh," said Tommy. "Have you met the Count?" he asked Joann.

"You mean the one who counts numbers?" said Joann.

"No," said John. "Tommy's talking about our captain. Not the captain of this ship, the one on our ship, *The Enchantress*."

"No, I haven't met either captain so far. But I'd like to."

The door to the game room opened, and a small, well-dressed woman with black hair in a bun and large brown eyes entered the room. The boys stopped talking and stood up.

"Miss Lawrence? I'm Marie Belton. I see you've met my sons."

"Yes. We were just having a conversation about the Internet and *Sesame Street*."

"Oh, yes. Big Bird and all that. I'm afraid the boys don't know very much about it. We've been away on a cruise for some time, and they haven't seen much television. I'm sure you'll have many interesting things to tell and show them. I'll stay with them for the next hour while you settle in. Could you be back by, say, three o'clock?"

"Yes, of course," said Joann.

Joann took her leave. Where have these folks been cruising, outer space? She wondered. No Internet? Madras shirts? Sixties hairstyles? This is definitely going to be an interesting cruise.

CHAPTER 12

The Marble Arch Hotel
London, England
Sunday, December 19th, 8:00 A.M.

L ee had ordered room service for eight o'clock. He tipped the waiter a pound and closed the door, double-locking it again. He then examined the food carefully. God, I'm paranoid, he thought, wondering if he should call the front desk and ask for a food taster. He could remember restaurants in the States, especially a couple in Newark Airport in the late seventies, where having a food taster would have been a good idea. Before the major makeover in the 1980s, the main terminal could have served as a set for a World War II movie. The whole place felt like a strong wind could take it down. And the few restaurants it housed had, in turn, accommodated wildlife—some human, some not. Lee recalled a dinner there, if one could call it that, when one of the nonhuman inhabitants with a gray fur coat and a long tail had darted underneath his table.

Last night, he'd ordered an American Continental breakfast: orange juice, coffee, and pastry. He needed something familiar. But the pastry was a British scone, of course, and the coffee—he liked it strong, but one sip was enough. Liz, who'd recalled that she was in England, had made a better choice: tea. Lee enjoyed complaining about English cuisine, but the food and complaints were distractions that didn't work. His mind was on neither.

"Breakfast here already?" Liz pulled off her eyeshades. Lee had never worn the pair she'd bought for him many years before. He'd joked that he would wake up in the night and think that he'd gone blind.

"How'd you sleep?" he asked, still grimacing from the coffee.

"Not that well."

"Me, neither. I kept thinking about the guy at the station and the car at the airport." He paused. "Let's just get this thing over with." He handed Liz the cup of tea.

"Where's the honey?"

Lee passed it to her then sniffed the cream before pouring it in his coffee.

"Is it spoiled?"

"No, just checking." "For what?"

"Oh, hell. Nothing, Liz. I'm just a little . . . on edge this morning."

"Well, I'm feeling better about this trip. Looks like the sun's out. We'll do some sightseeing. Have some time together. . ."

Here she goes, Lee thought.

". . . go to a nice restaurant. Maybe do a little shopping before . . ."

Lee interrupted. "The main thing we've got to do today is pick up the package at three-thirty sharp."

"The package," said Liz, in a mocking tone. "I wonder what's in it."

"I have no idea, and I don't want to know."

He tried to weaken the coffee, which had the viscosity of oil, with more cream. Liz resumed her channel surfing from the previous night.

"I think I'll go down to the lobby and see if they have *The Times*." As soon as he closed the door, he felt a familiar craving that he hadn't experienced in months and wondered if the lobby bar was open. He hadn't had a drink since the accident. The police officer, who knew him, didn't give him a sobriety test; he just wrote up the incident as a minor, single-car accident. Black ice. Driving too fast following a couple of drinks with Dr. Forester after work, he skidded off the road and took out the headlight and fender on the passenger side. It was a wake-up call, and he heeded it.

Lee didn't get on the elevator. He went back to the room.

"No *Times*?" asked Liz.

"No, I didn't go," said Lee, returning to his coffee.

"You don't look so good. Did you sleep at all?"

"Not much."

"What are you thinking about?"

"The changes we've made in the last few years since I got back."

After being away for so many months, he had difficulty restarting his practice and his life. All he told people, all that he *could* tell people, was that he'd been away working on his book and got caught up in the accident at the Pine Grove nuclear plant, and that his return was delayed because the government somehow had the mistaken idea that he and his friend Angus had something to do with the accident. But the people of Winterpool thought that there was more to it than that. There had been rumors. Small-town rumors: Liz and Lee had separated because of another woman. Or Lee had been undergoing treatment for a cancer caused by the nuclear accident.

Lee knew a lot about rumors and how destructive they could be in a small town. He'd grown up hearing the stories about his great-uncle Bush from his mother. He'd been driven out of his home and into the Appalachian woods by rumors that he'd killed a young woman and her husband. He hadn't, but he stayed in the woods, became a hermit. Years passed. But the stories only got larger and more frightening. People were afraid of Uncle Bush.

"Being alone," Lee's mom would say, "gave Uncle Bush plenty of time to think and hope." He decided that he would create an even bigger story than those the townspeople were telling. But he also wanted to hear their stories before he died — or, as they would say in those days, "got low." So, with the help of the town undertaker, he arranged for his own funeral—a funeral that would be preached before his death.

Lee had always thought that his uncle must have had a lot of hope to try such a thing. It was the middle of the Great Depression. But the funeral director and some of the townspeople saw the opportunity to create some publicity for themselves and their town, and an opportunity, of course, to make some money. Lee smiled, remembering all of this. He guessed that rumors *could* lead to something positive. Uncle Bush got to hear the townspeople's stories and to tell his own. His funeral was a great success. Hundreds came, including Lee's mother and father. It made national news and his story was eventually made into a movie, *Get Low*, with Robert Duval playing "crazy" or optimistic Uncle Bush, depending on how you thought about it.

So, it hadn't been easy for Lee, even with the help of friends like Griff, who insisted that he spend time on his fishing boat, or old friends who visited them when the demands of their lives allowed.

The drinking had been a refuge. Just a couple. No harm in that. Every evening. And then one at lunch. And the weekends. Another bottle of wine—or two or three? Liz and Lee had argued about the drinking, but Lee hadn't listened to her until the accident.

"You know, Liz, I don't know what would happen when I came back from Boston."

Liz smiled. "Well, I wasn't sure that we would ever *get* you back from Boston." She switched off the television.

"I know, but—but I mean with us. Dru out of the house. Retirement." He looked down at the floor. "Well, partial retirement. Just you and me." He looked at Liz. "I didn't know if we could . . ." he hesitated, "if we could make it."

Liz didn't say anything.

"But now I'm feeling pretty good about our chances. About us. You know, we seem to argue less. Our . . . timing with each other is better."

"It's still not the greatest sometimes," said Liz.

"And other things are better, too," said Lee with assurance.

"You mean sex?"

"Well, that too." he replied with a smile.

"Why is that, Lee?" she said, looking directly into his eyes. "I haven't changed that much."

"I guess I've changed the way I think about all of that." "What do you mean?"

"I didn't want to change." Lee looked away. "I didn't want to accept the way things were. How I needed to change. But flexibility is a good thing." He chuckled. "Hmm. You've got to change your thinking before you can change what you're doing." He paused. "I guess I finally took my own advice."

"Well, I'm glad I'm married to a flexible man." She put her arms around Lee, pulling him back into the bed, and kissed him. Really kissed him.

"So why don't we practice what we preach?" And they did.

The sun rose higher as the morning passed. The maid's knock at the door roused them around noon. They showered and started to dress. Lee asked her again not to go with him. And predictably, Liz refused. They decided to try the park again. This time there were no men in trench coats. The sun felt warm. They sat on a park bench and stared silently at the sky.

"Honey, it's almost three. We'd best get a taxi. Let's walk over to Paddington and catch one."

Before they could reach the station, Lee waved one down on Edgeware. "The Tower of London," he instructed the cabbie.

"Right. Straight away," said the young driver.

Located in central London, on the north bank of the Thames, the Tower is a complex of buildings and towers that have served as a fortress; royal palace; and prison used most famously by Henry the Eighth to confine one of his wives, Anne Boleyn. In 1078, William the Conqueror built the first tower, the White Tower.

Traffic was heavy. As they approached the Cannon Street Station, a truck suddenly pulled out of a side street, narrowly missing the cab. Liz screamed. The driver's quick response averted a crash that might have killed all three of them.

"I'm sorry, sir. I don't know where that bloke came from. Are you okay, ma'am?"

"Yes, I'm fine," said Liz, regaining her composure. Her face was flushed.

Lee didn't speak. He just looked at Liz. They both knew what had just happened, but they silently agreed that talking about it at that very moment would do them no good.

The driver dropped them at the Tower tube station, apologizing again. Lee gave him a good tip, and he and Liz walked toward the entrance gate.

The Tower was clearly a fortress between two concentric circles of defensive walls and a moat. Even in the bright afternoon sunlight, it was foreboding.

"You know, this place has ghosts. Anne Boleyn, who was finally beheaded by her loving husband Henry, has been seen walking around the White Tower carrying her head under her arm," said Lee.

"Please, Lee, no bad jokes about a woman losing her head over a man," said Liz, looking for signage. "Where are we going?"

Lee was thumbing through the *Authoritative Guide to London.* "It says that the museum is near the center of the complex." They walked on toward the White Tower. The Museum of the Royal Regiment of Fusiliers, City of London Regiment, was in a building off the main courtyard.

"Is it time?"

"Almost." He paused. "You can wait out here."

"No way! I'm going with you. The whole place gives me a chill."

"Hey, you're the one who insisted on coming." They walked on. "Relax. The last execution was in 1601."

"Are you forgetting the one a few minutes ago, for which we were almost the guests of honor?"

Lee smiled. "Well, in that case, would you like to see the Crown Jewels before we leave?"

"I think I saw them this morning." Lee chuckled. "There's the museum entrance. The ticket clerk is supposed to tell me where the package is. Here goes nothing."

They walked past a sign apologizing for the lack of access for persons with disabilities. Liz trailed behind Lee, who approached the ticket booth and placed a ten-pound note on the counter. The clerk slid the change and two tickets through the opening in the glass. Lee waited. The clerk said nothing. When Lee didn't move, the clerk pointed to the tickets. Lee picked them up and waited. The man pointed at the tickets again. Lee looked at them again and back at the clerk. The clerk took the tickets out of Lee's hand and turned them over, exposing a handwritten note on the back of one. Lee nodded. He was sure that he'd never have made it as a secret agent.

He turned to Liz. "Okay," he said with a sigh, and they entered the museum. The note on the back of the ticket said, *Under the right corner of the portrait of Field Marshal Sir Edward Blakeney.*

"What do you want me to do?" whispered Liz.

"Just help me find this guy," said Lee, as he started to scan the walls. "You know, I think someone doesn't want us to pick up this package."

"I think you're right, Sherlock," said Liz as she looked for a nameplate on one of the portraits. "Boy, this place is low tech. No cameras that I can see. How about this one?" she asked.

"No, that's Lord Dartmouth," said Lee, looking at the *Visitor's Guide*. There was no shortage of battle-scene portraits, but, finally, on the back wall, they found the right one. Sir Edward Blakeney, fourteenth Colonel of the Royal Fusiliers.

Even though the museum was empty of visitors, Liz stood guard.

"Doesn't look like there's any alarm wiring attached to the painting."

Lee felt for the package behind the portrait's frame.

"Sour-looking fellow," said Liz, staring at the portrait.

Lee nodded, but his attention was on the frame.

"Who could want to steal this guy?" groaned Liz.

"The damn thing must be awfully small," said Lee as he ran his hand across the back of the portrait.

"Hurry up, Lee. They're going to close."

"I'm hurrying . . . here, I think I've got something." Lee pulled out a CD case and read the title, "Greatest Hits of Rock 'n Roll, Volume I." He put his hand behind the frame again and felt the right corner. "Nothing else." He looked at Liz and shrugged. "I guess this is it." He slipped the CD into his coat pocket. They tried not to look guilty, nodding and smiling at the ticket clerk as they left the museum.

"No more sightseeing for today, right?" asked Lee, as they walked toward the Tower Hill entrance.

"What do you think?"

They pushed through the crowd that was gathering for the Beefeaters, the Tower guards' Ceremony of the Keys, which they performed every evening to secure the Tower for the night.

As they exited the last tower, a raven swooped past them.

"Is that a good sign or a bad sign? I can't remember," asked Lee.

"Something about being by your window…"

Liz wasn't paying attention. Her mind was on getting back to the hotel. "Let's take the Underground. I've had enough with taxis for today."

The tube station was clean. The train was on time. And they weren't being followed.

"So, I take it we're staying in tonight?" asked Lee, as they stepped into the hotel elevator.

"I don't understand you sometimes, Lee. One minute you're wired and paranoid, and the next you're doing a comedy routine. I think we've had our share of luck for the day. Let's not push it."

"Well, some days things just reach a point that the only thing you can do is laugh," said Lee, trying not to sound defensive.

Liz didn't respond.

The room was warm; they'd left the heat up. The bed felt soft as Lee kicked off his shoes and laid down across it.

"I'm hungry," he said. "Let's order something from room service." He thought about how good a beer would taste. The craving was still there.

Room service was slow, even though their order was small and not very exciting. Fish and chips. Lee ordered bottled water. The craving started to pass. When the meal finally arrived, his appetite had also passed. They both sat in front of the television and watched BBC news. New fighting in Baghdad. More car bombs.

After the news, Liz pulled out her mystery novel. Lee skimmed through the *AAA Guide to London* that he'd bought a few weeks before. They made two phone calls before getting ready for bed. Liz called Val and made arrangements to meet her the next morning at Harrod's. Lee called Dru.

"How are you, honey?"

"Dad, I'm great! I miss you guys. Hope you're relaxing and enjoying London."

"Oh, we are." Little did she know.

"You need to retire, Dad. I mean, really retire."

"Yeah, yeah, I know, but . . . well—we'll talk about it . . . again. How's your boyfriend?"

"Rob, Dad. He just got that job with Marine Resources that he applied for months ago. Took forever." Rob had been out of college since graduation but with no job. He'd finally found work in his field, which was considerably better than the thousands of college graduates who hadn't.

"Well, I'm glad to hear he's working, especially in this economy."

"We have to talk with you and mom when you get back." "What about?" said Lee, sounding alarmed.

"Well, our plans."

Lee took a deep breath. "Your plans? That sounds serious." "Well, yes, I think we are."

Lee wasn't quite sure what to say.

"Well, that's great, honey. We'll talk when we get back. We'll have plenty of time during the holidays to do that. Here's your mom."

Lee shook his head and mouthed, "don't ask" and handed the phone to Liz, who immediately began to discuss the shopping trip that she was planning with Val. By the time the phone call ended,

Lee had paced around the room three or four times.

"Well?" Liz asked.

"Well, what?"

"I know," said Liz. "They've been talking about marriage."

"Well?"

"We'll talk with them over the holidays. There's not much we can do but listen. She's an adult, a responsible one."

That satisfied Lee, at least for the moment. They took turns in the bathroom and talked briefly about the next day. Lee would take the mid- morning Eurostar out of St. Paneras Station. He'd have time to think about his only daughter and her boyfriend . . . fiancé . . . on the Eurostar.

About ten o'clock, Liz turned the light off. Lee lay awake for a long time: Jet lag, men in brown trench coats, large trucks, and Dru. When he finally fell into a deep sleep, he dreamed of an early fall evening, many years ago, when they had walked the Boulevard around Back Cove in Portland. That evening, they decided to adopt. Liz had had a miscarriage. They were both in their early forties. The decision had taken them a while to make, but it was a good one. A few months later, Dru was in their arms, and now . . . she was going to get married and start a family of her own.

CHAPTER 13

The Marble Arch
London, England
Monday, December 20th, 7:30 A.M.

*Hope is the thing with feathers that perches in the soul and
sings the tune without the words, and never stops at all.*

~ Emily Dickinson

Their wake-up call came at 7:30 A.M. Liz groaned and rolled over. Lee sat up on the edge of the bed for a minute but then rejoined her. At eight o'clock, he got to his feet and headed to the bathroom. Another sunny day. Lee felt hopeful. Sunlight and warm water. God, we really are the children of Mother Nature, he thought as he turned off the shower.

Liz was up and feeling equally optimistic about the day. "Perhaps this little favor we're doing for Jennings is a good thing," she said as she took possession of the bathroom.

"It certainly doesn't hurt to look at it that way. We Americans are used to exporting hope, not fear," he shouted through the door.

Their conversation was interrupted by a knock at the door. "Room service," said the voice.

"Breakfast is served," shouted Lee. He didn't wait for Liz. He had a quick cup of coffee, some OJ, and a scone that wasn't as bad as he remembered from the day before.

Lee was ready to go as Liz emerged from the bathroom. She looked at Lee and "the thing."

"You're not taking that with you," said Liz.

Lee grimaced. "Well, yes," he said.

"I think we should switch bags. Mine is much smaller. It'll be easier for you." Liz started for the closet to get her bag. Lee looked unconvinced and didn't move.

"It'll only take a minute," said Liz. "Relax."

Rather than complaining, he realized that Liz was right, as she often was. He told her that her suggestion was a good one and helped her repack his bag. He also gave himself extra points on the change scale.

Lee tucked "the package" in a pocket in his briefcase. He assumed that it would go safely through customs and security. It looked like an ordinary CD, which were getting rarer all the time. Maybe it was an ordinary CD with secret information coded behind the music or on the CD instead of music. What did he know? He hugged Liz and kissed her forehead.

"No," she said. "A real kiss."

Lee stepped back and looked at her then took her in his arms and kissed her like it might be their last. He tried to reassure her that all would be well by mumbling something to that effect, and they both pretended it would be.

He caught a taxi in front of the hotel. The taxi driver, like most British drivers, engaged him in conversation.

"Your first time with the Eurostar?"

"Yes. I've been looking forward to it."

"I believe you'll be impressed with the terminal. Much like Grand Central Station in New York." St. Paneras International was an old train station restored to its earlier glory.

"Yes, I've heard. The longest champagne bar in Europe." The craving was still there.

"Yes, sir. The longest in the U.K. and in Europe," the driver corrected.

Lee had read the AAA guide and knew other bits of trivia. "It's been in a number of films," he offered, enjoying the distraction of the conversation.

"Yes, sir. It was a stand-in for King's Crossing Platform nine and three quarters in *Harry Potter*."

The station was, indeed, beautiful. Check-in was easy, and Lee went through security without delay. He checked for the CD when he retrieved his briefcase. The package had made it too.

The train was on time. Lee's seat was in Car 5, a standard-class car. He never saw the point in spending additional money on business class. It was next to a bar car, not that he was planning on having a drink. Ah, the "good ole days," he mumbled, "when a Jack Daniel's Manhattan could quickly dull any feeling that might be giving me difficulty."

The trip to Paris would take approximately two-and-a-half hours. They would be under the Channel for only twenty minutes. The train was amazingly quiet and not crowded.

The trip to Paris was for a WHO conference on "Optimism." After all these years, medicine had figured out that "our explanatory style" has a direct impact on our health, that how we look at the world can make us sick or help us get well, that our perception of things is the key.

But Lee's mind wasn't on the conference details. He was having his own internal debate about optimism and pessimism. On the side of pessimism were his friends Bill and Rick, and his old boss Dennis. And on the side of optimism were his mother and his Aunt Rose.

After detention in Boston, he'd committed himself to the practice of gratitude, but that had been a hard promise to keep. With Vietnam, Grenada, Desert Storm, Iraq, and Afghanistan in his lifetime, it seemed like America was interminably at war. And the effects were pervasive. We filled our televisions and video games with violence. Our economy seemed to demand that wars continue. Lee had difficulty remembering his mother's words: "Son, just always remember, good or bad, this too will pass." She'd been born before World War I and had lived through the Depression, World War II, the Korean Conflict, Vietnam, and the Iraq war.

But blame was an easy thing. An incompetent federal administration, baby-boomers who sold out, young people who seemed more interested in texting and smartphones than in the actual world. But then he would remember his aunt: "Lee, you've got to focus on what you have, not what you don't." God knows, she'd learned that lesson well, having lived through the death of two husbands then dying herself just short of her sixtieth birthday. Even with advanced degrees in psychiatry and psychology, his friends and old boss were no match for two women who understood life by living it to the fullest.

Two hours passed quickly. Lee almost missed the Channel crossing. It seemed very much like all the other train tunnels he'd been through, just longer.

He found himself thinking more about his mother and her stories. One of the most romantic and certainly one filled with hope for the future was about Aunt Ollie and Uncle Clyde's marriage. They'd grown up in Lee's hometown and had been engaged, but, for some reason—neither Lee nor his mother knew what—the engagement ended. Clyde moved to Chicago and made a life for himself. Ollie stayed and married, but her husband died in the 1930s. She remained a widow for the next twenty-five years.

One summer day in 1956, Clyde returned. His life in Chicago had been a good one. He'd married and had a son. But when his wife died, he decided to return to find Ollie. And he did.

She hadn't heard from him in ten years and was reluctant to "court." After all, they were both in their late sixties. Ollie knew that people in their small southern town would consider them ridiculous. They would talk. But Clyde was persuasive. He soon proposed, and they married.

Lee didn't remember much of this. He'd been just ten or eleven. He did remember the wedding, because he was the ring-bearer. They were married at Lee's home, and his parents served as witnesses.

He also remembered the years that followed. The two clearly

enjoyed each other. Ollie, who had been ill—Lee's father called her a hypochondriac—suddenly returned to good health, and Clyde seemed to find new energy and purpose. Ollie died in 1968, and Clyde followed her within a year.

Lee wondered why they had suddenly come to mind. Perhaps because thinking about his mother and the love that Ollie and Clyde had shared was certainly a nice diversion from the present. Lee wasn't at all sure what awaited him in Paris. He thought about the near miss at the airport, the man in the trench coat, and the truck that almost demolished their taxi.

The train arrived at the Paris Nord Station on time. Again, customs was quick and easy, which usually worried Lee. What if the bad guys got through as easily as he did? But he wouldn't think about that today. He was in Paris. He'd only been in the city a couple of times, but he loved it. Even though he spoke very little French, he was comfortable there. The pace, the feel of the city, was different from New York or London. Slower, saner.

The cab ride to the Ambassador was short. The old hotel was in the center of the Opera District, a few minutes from the Opera Garnier and the Moulin Rouge. Built in the 1920s, it retained its art deco theme. Lee didn't especially like the couches or chairs in the lobby or find them comfortable, but the choice of color and their arrangement worked. It wouldn't have worked, Lee thought, if an American had designed it. The hotel would have looked like a Disney-style brothel, but the French somehow made it work.

And the Lindbergh Bar, Humphrey Bogart and Ingrid Bergman— a couple whose timing, when combined with World War II, just didn't work—Claude Rains and the Foreign Legion. Lee smiled from the memory of the 1940s classic film *Casablanca*. He always found welcome distraction in that fantasy.

He thought again of the trip to Paris for Dru's sixteenth birthday—a short trip, only a week. They'd wanted to stay longer, but Paris was expensive, especially when the dollar hit a new low and stayed there.

Lee believed that the desk clerk had been at the hotel even then. Lee's French was terrible, but the clerk appreciated his efforts. Yes, he had worked at the hotel for over twenty years, and, yes, he thought that he might remember Lee and his family. At least that's what he said. Lee's hook usually did make an impression.

Lee settled into his room, unpacked, and called Liz, who was having a great time with Val. She had stayed within the budget they'd set for the trip. "Well, almost," she admitted. There was just one thing. A handbag she knew "Dru would love." She knew Lee wouldn't object if it was for Dru.

"And?" she asked.

"Nothing yet from the Rock 'n Roll Hall of Fame, but I'll keep you posted."

It was 4:30. Lee searched the room for a note. Nothing. No phone calls or messages. He channel surfed, watched some television, and checked his Gmail. He took a nap then showered just to wake up. He still had jet lag.

He had an uneventful meal at the hotel—a veal dish that he couldn't pronounce, but he tried, and the waiter smiled. He thought about a walk after dinner. Maybe down to Galleries Lafayette. He checked his watch. It was after six. It would be closed. The French believed that evenings were for things other than shopping. He finally ended up in the bar.

"Tonic and lime, *sil vous plait.*" He was sure that the bartender took offense. He waited. Sipped his drink. But there was no message written on his cocktail napkin. He went back to the room. No messages. No notes. No calls. No emails. No texts. No one appeared interested in telling him what to do with the *Greatest Hits of Rock 'n Roll.*

More television and a look at the workshop agenda for tomorrow rounded out the evening. A chair propped against the door, and lights out. He closed the drapes, and the City of Lights disappeared. Maybe a note would appear in his granola in the morning. He'd have to remember to look before he poured the milk.

Before Lee drifted off to sleep, he thought of Jean, and the sadness came, as it always did. Jean was a woman he had been . . .yes, in love with for most of his life. They'd met in graduate school. After completing her doctorate, she moved to Europe. Lee still had his internship to do. They'd seen each other a number of times—even talked about marriage. But, like Bogey and Bergman, their timing never worked, and long-distance relationships were hard to maintain. They'd both married, lost touch. Just Christmas cards. Her husband died in 2022, and she returned to the States for a visit, just in time to become embroiled in Lou's Boston mess. She'd tried to help. Since Boston, they'd written only a few times. Jennings had discouraged Gmail or phone calls. But Lee's paranoia was the main reason. He was sure that the feds were monitoring their communications, and maybe they were, so even their letters said little. But he still thought of her.

Exhausted, he finally slept. He dreamed but had no memory of it when he awoke the next morning at seven.

CHAPTER 14

Home of Jefferson Davis Powell, his wife, and three children
Durham, North Carolina
Monday, December 20, 20th, 10:15 A.M.

Now faith is confidence in what we hope for
and assurance about what we do not see.

~ Hebrews

Jeff had been out of work for nine months. His unemployment benefits had run out. His home was facing foreclosure. His wife Judy worked, but only part time.

He was looking at his computer and holding something in his hand that he had printed off. "Judy, I've got some good news."

His wife of ten years was slow to respond. She was sitting on the couch folding laundry. He'd had good news before. Finally, she spoke. "I hope so. Are you sure?"

"TransSea has a job for me. They've attached an airline ticket."

"Pretty sure of themselves, aren't they?" She realized what he was saying.

"Does this mean you'll be in Texas for the holidays?"

"No, Bermuda."

"Bermuda?"

"Yeah."

They both looked puzzled. When Jeff had returned from Afghanistan, TransSea was one of the few companies that offered him employment. He worked on the Gulf rigs for numerous years. It was hard, dangerous work, but it paid well. Judy prayed every night that God would protect him. She was a very religious person.

Unfortunately, he was a subcontract employee, so, when he was injured, the help he got from TransSea's subcontractor was very little. They ran out of money. Jeff was forced to settle with the workers' comp carrier and to take what work he could.

"I don't know, Jeff. I don't trust those people. They didn't treat you very good when you got hurt. What are they doing in Bermuda?"

"I don't know. It's an awfully big company. They've got an office there. They want to meet me there tomorrow evening."

She shook her head. "I don't like the way that sounds." She looked down at the laundry and stopped folding.

Jeff got up and walked over to the couch. He put his arm around her. "But they've always paid me well, and we need the money." He smiled. "They say they're sure I have the skills to do the job." He waited.

Judy touched his cheek lovingly. "Okay, honey. I'll trust your judgment this time."

CHAPTER 15

Senator Clayton's Office, Hart Office Building
Washington, DC
Monday, December 20th, 10:33 A.M.

Optimist: Someone who tells you to cheer
up when things are going his way.

~ Edward R. Murrow

"I know. I know, Fred. We have no chance of preventing Hollocore from getting the contract. But Senator Greenwood and I are still voting against it."

Fred Bolin, her Chief of Staff, looked away and said dismissively, "I'm sure you feel that you have to vote your conviction."

"Fred, look at me. This is really important. It's probably the most important thing I've ever dealt with in my whole political career. Some one or some thing has to stop Hollocore."

"I know, Senator. I just don't know who or what is going to be able to do that. Chambers has half the committee in his back pocket. Your colleagues are frightened of him. I don't think they'll risk crossing him."

"But, Fred, you saw that recent poll. Most of the American people would favor what I'm proposing. Most people would welcome an opportunity to slow things down. To think about what we're doing before we do it. It's corporations like Hollocore that are full-speed ahead and damn the torpedoes."

Fred nodded in agreement.

"And what do you know about TransSea?" she asked.

"Not much. They've been around a few years. They're privately held. They're in the energy business like Hollocore, and they're Hollocore's main competitor. But they seem different in their approach to things."

"How so?"

"Well, from what I've heard, they treat their employees well. They don't seem totally motivated by greed. In fact, they've worked fairly closely with the Environmental Protection Agency on the wells they operate in the Gulf. And their management team is a bit of a mystery. It's not a company run by personalities. They certainly don't have anyone like Dick Chambers leading the charge."

"Do you realize what could happen with this supercomputer in the hands of someone like Chambers? He's a real piece of work."

Fred chuckled. "As my old daddy would say, 'I wouldn't trust him in an outhouse with a muzzle on.'"

She laughed. "Fred, where do you come up with those sayings? Or should I say, where did your daddy come up with those sayings?"

Nancy Clayton had always tried to act on her convictions, but each year, doing so seemed more difficult. She had come up through the ranks. Six terms in the House, and now she was the Junior Senator from California. This business of being a presidential candidate seemed to make it even harder. Party leadership told her not to fight losing battles. They weren't sure that she wouldn't self-destruct before Election Day, and she wasn't either. But the election was a long way off; she had to get the nomination first.

Fred Bolin wasn't sure that he wanted her to get the nomination. For the first time in all the years he'd worked for her, he was ambivalent about her campaign. He wasn't sure that winning the nomination or even winning the presidency would be what she really wanted. She had wanted a good marriage and her family, but politics, he felt, had robbed her of both.

Now in his late fifties, he'd worked for her first in California. Then he followed her to DC. He never married. Her career was his life.

He could write a book about Nancy Clayton. From a small

town in the Midwest, she'd worked to put herself through college. Her mother was a passive woman, perhaps because she had a physical disability and felt that she had few choices. Her father was hardworking but distant.

Nancy earned a Bachelor's degree from an Ivy League school but had to live at home and commute to do it. She was a Catholic in a school primarily made up of students from "old money" Protestant homes. That was when Fred met her. He was one of those students.

To survive, she learned to be a good politician, to negotiate. She got a law degree and met her husband in law school.

When Fred finished college, he took a job in the family firm. He didn't have to. He had a trust fund. His parents seemed uninterested in what he did. When he performed poorly in college, they wrote him off, ignored him, certain that he wouldn't live up to his "potential."

To his amazement, one late May afternoon, Nancy Clayton showed up at his office to intern for the summer. She didn't ignore him. They rekindled their old friendship. Brian, her boyfriend from law school was now her fiancé, and they married soon after she finished her law degree. Fred followed her to a law firm in San Francisco. She was a rising star, and he rose with her.

She wanted it all. When she gave birth to a daughter in her mid-thirties, Fred became a part-time babysitter and surrogate parent. She wasn't there enough, Fred felt, when Kimberly needed her. When Kimberly got into trouble in her early teens, Fred helped to cover it up. Unlike Nancy, Brian didn't even try to be there for his daughter. Like Fred's parents had, he wrote Kimberly off when she needed him most.

Brian was a womanizer and a drinker. Fred knew that from the beginning, but Nancy wouldn't hear of it. She threw herself into her work and continued to deny that he was involved with other women and had a drinking problem. She focused her attention— what limited attention she had for her family—on her daughter. Kimberly returned to college and, like her mom, met a guy. Unlike her mom, she got pregnant immediately. Getting pregnant had been a struggle for Nancy, both making the decision and then being able to make it happen. But not for her daughter. Nancy was about to be a grandparent. Excited about this prospect, she decided to fly back to the coast to tell Brian, hoping that it might draw the family together. When her afternoon committee meeting on the hill was cancelled, she took an earlier flight and found Brian in bed with another woman. It was finally enough.

She filed for divorce and never looked back. At least that's what she was fond of saying. She again concentrated on her work. That was okay with Fred; he got to see her more.

When she'd first brought up the presidential nomination, Fred had tried to talk her out of it. But some days, it seemed to be the only thing that kept her from giving up. It was sad, he felt, for it to come to that. Could he have given her more than Brian? Brian was a man's man. Handsome, a sharp dresser, and a risk taker. All the things that Fred wasn't.

He fantasized about telling her how he felt, but he never had and assumed that he never would. She liked him. She cared about him, like a good employer cares about a good employee. But was there more there than that? He didn't know and most likely would never find out.

CHAPTER 16

The Ambassador Hotel
Paris, France
Tuesday, December 21st, 8:16 A.M.

God is with those who are patient.

~The Koran

The Continental breakfast that came with the room was in a salon off the main dining room: Pastry—no scones—dry cereal, breads, fruit, and lots of stewed prunes. The French knew about the gastric consequences of international travel. Lee chose the stewed prunes, coffee, orange juice, a croissant, and granola—without a secret message—and yesterday's *New York Times.* Hard copies of a newspaper were hard to find, so he would have to be pleased with yesterday's news.

The front page held the usual reports of bombings in Baghdad and rocket attacks in Israel, and a fairly long article about "UFO Mania." Evidently, people globally were reporting sightings. As usual, authorities discounted them as just weather balloons, the planet Venus, the Northern Lights, etc. The article concluded by saying that no one had ever presented hard evidence of the existence of alien lifeforms.

Well, I'm not sure of that, Lee thought.

There was also an article about Senator Clayton's campaign, including endorsements from some of the Old Guard, even though it was still early in the campaign. The country was desperate for new leadership. But what were average people willing to do? Were we just looking for another savior whom we would reject after six months when he or she couldn't deliver all the items on our wish list?

As Lee started to tuck the paper under his arm, another article caught his attention: "TransSea and Hollocore Vie for Contract to Build Supercomputer." The EU and UK, the original developers of this project, had fallen on hard times and were looking to the United States for a new partner and funding. The US had agreed to take on the final phase of the project. The American answer to the funding issue, of course, was to privatize the project and look for corporate partners.

The article extolled the possible benefits of developing a supercomputer, like curing the ills of old age. If that weren't enough, humans might someday be immortal by merging with computers.

Lee shook his head. Merging with a computer: wish fulfillment on a grand scale for some people, I suppose. Cyborg mania! He chuckled.

The article didn't mention Senator Clayton and said nothing about the ethical challenges that the human race would confront if we developed such a computer. Instead, it focused on the competition between TransSea and Hollocore to obtain the contract to build it. The companies had been bitter rivals for years.

Merging with a computer? That's sure as hell one thing I wouldn't want to do. And life extension? Whose life would be extended? And whose wouldn't? Who would decide? The computer? The morning paper hadn't put Lee in a good mood.

Registration for the WHO meeting was on the eighth floor. He didn't recognize anyone in the hall outside the meeting room. He picked up his registration packet and found a seat at a table near the back of the room. A small group, maybe fifty. The program was billed as an update on current research on optimism, but the focus was on integrating the concepts of explanatory style into the day-to-day practice of medicine.

The program began promptly at nine o'clock. The group was a mix of practitioners, mostly from the United States and the United Kingdom, and an assortment of public health types, mainly from

Western Europe. In the final years before his "retirement," he'd worked on an educational project in which one of the main components was optimism. An old friend at the American Psychological Association had arranged for his invitation.

Selling prevention to the healthcare industry had always been difficult, as the first speaker pointed out. There were usually no drug prescriptions that needed writing or refilling repeatedly, expensive equipment to sell, or procedures to bill out. The profit margin for prevention was small. Very small. And healthcare was a for-profit venture, especially in the States.

But signs of hope existed, the second speaker maintained. The UK had been investing heavily in training practitioners in cognitive behavioral approaches to treating depression rather than spending millions on psychotropic medications. Discussion was active and, at times, heated. Lee enjoyed it, almost forgetting his other purpose in being there. The morning session ended at 10:30. The luncheon wouldn't begin until 12:30. Then more speakers and recognitions. There was time, Lee thought, for a walk to see a bit of Paris.

The registration area was crowded and noisy. The elevators were straight ahead. He didn't think he'd need an overcoat so decided not to go back to his room. As he waited for the elevator, he saw the Eiffel Tower out of the corner of his eye. The elevator was crowded, but people gradually exited. Everyone seemed in a hurry. The holidays. The door opened and Lee crossed the lobby. The doorman smiled.

"*Monsieur,* taxi?"

"Um," Lee hesitated. "*Oui.* The Eiffel Tower." The driver nodded.

A walk would be better for his health. He needed the exercise, he thought, but slipped into the cab anyway. It was a beautiful late December morning. Sunny, though a bit windy, which made it feel colder. Traffic was heavy. The shops were busy. Last-minute shoppers like Lee. He hadn't finished his list. He'd waited for Paris. Something special this year for both Liz and his daughter. He would have time for that this evening or tomorrow morning. But what? Which shop?

Bebe for his daughter, the shop she'd loved on her first trip to Paris.

Lee was so occupied with his shopping list and thoughts that he didn't give much credence to the black BMW that had been following his cab since the hotel. Lee didn't even notice when the cab stopped.

"*Monsieur*?"

"Oh, yes. I mean, *oui*. We're here. Right?'

The driver rolled his eyes. "*Oui, monsieur.*" Lee was sure that he was thinking something about Americans. Lee handed him what he thought was the fare and a tip. The driver nodded.

The tower wasn't crowded. A ticket to the top required no conversation; given his French, he was thankful. He boarded the elevator with a group of Japanese tourists. The gate clanged shut, and the elevator slowly began to move. It creaked, groaned, and swayed some in the wind.

The viewing platform wasn't crowded, either. Lee walked around it slowly. The usual assortment of young and some not-so-young lovers seemed to hardly notice the cold, but the weather discouraged a long stay. He looked out over the city. The *Arc de Triomphe*, he was sure of that. The *Louvre,* maybe. It was getting cold. He looked at his watch. Later than he thought, 11:48. The traffic would be even worse on the way back.

Then he saw her. He aborted his retreat to the elevator. She was standing by herself. The hair, still blond, thanks to, as she would say, "better living through chemistry." The coat, a dress, even on such a cold day, an umbrella. A petite woman.

The last time he'd seen Jean was in Paris. Jennings had arranged for them to spend a few hours together. They had one meal together, a dinner, then it was over. Jennings saw to that. No, it wasn't at the Eiffel Tower, although they'd talked of meeting there someday: *An Affair to Remember*, with the Eiffel Tower rather than the Empire State Building. Business had brought Lee to Paris three years ago. Another WHO meeting and a "delivery" for Jennings. A relatively uncomplicated delivery, but, again, one he hadn't felt that he could turn down. He hadn't told Liz about seeing Jean. He and Jean met at the *Café de la Paix* for a simple dinner, a few drinks, and a lot of reminiscing. She was seeing a friend of her late husband's, a man named Carl. They toasted their separate lives and their relationship. "Like a rock," she said. It had been worn by the years but hadn't washed away.

Lee started to walk toward her, but a man about his age hurried past him and touched the woman on the shoulder. She turned. Lee waited. She was now facing Lee, but the man, a large man, white hair, tall, slim—slimmer than Lee—blocked his view. Finally, the man moved. It wasn't Jean.

He was shaking. From the cold, he told himself. He rubbed his arms and stamped his feet and finally forced himself in the direction of the elevator. As he had decided many years before, we must simply accept some things, even if we never understand them.

CHAPTER 17

The Eiffel Tower
Paris, France
Tuesday, December 21st

The real jihad is the warfare against the passions.

~AL-GHAZAH,
MUSLIM WRITER

W hen Lee reached the ground, he focused on getting back to the meeting. The black car from earlier was still there, waiting near the cabstand. He wasn't in the mood and considered confronting the occupants but thought better of it.

The ride back to the hotel was uneventful. Lee tried to keep his focus. The meeting. The delivery. Some shopping for family. Home.

The BMW pulled past the cab at the hotel's entrance. Lee waved.

He quickly crossed the lobby and squeezed onto the elevator with fifteen others. After stopping at what seemed like every floor, he finally arrived at the one on which the afternoon meeting was being held. He walked past the registration table. Five minutes to spare, he thought.

"*Monsieur!*" The young French woman overseeing the registration table was waving him over. She handed Lee a sealed envelope.

"*Merci,*" said Lee. At last maybe he could get this over today and enjoy the rest of the meeting and the trip home. He opened the envelope.

Dr. Brazil – Your life is in danger. You must leave the hotel now! Do not return to your room. Go to the hotel basement, B-1. Exit through the staff entrance. A car will be waiting for you. You will be driven to one of the side entrances to the Cathedral of Notre

Dame. Go in. Lose yourself in the crowd. I will find you. ~ Andy

Lee hesitated. He read the note again. He'd brought his appointment calendar—a hard copy rarity these days—and, of course, the package. He really didn't need to return to his room.

For a moment, he felt angry: I'm too old for this *I Spy* business! But his old friend fear began to push up and propel him toward the elevator. The doors opened. He stepped in. They closed. He was alone. He hesitated again then pushed B-1. The elevator groaned past the floors. The doors finally opened again. A maid pushing a cart filled with clean linen hurried into the elevator.

Lee stepped off the elevator and peered down the long hall. He could see the outline of an entrance. He assumed that this was the right one. He looked back. The hall was deserted.

He began to walk slowly down the hall, but his pace quickened. Light poured into the building from a door at the end of the hall. It partially blinded him. He couldn't see what was to his left or right. He could hear machinery, he assumed washers and dryers, in process. He tried to read door signs as he passed, but stress rendered his French nonexistent.

By the time he reached the door, he was jogging and half out of breath. He hit the crash bar and the door sprang open with a jolt. A black limousine sat at the foot of the loading ramp. Lee walked down the steps toward the nondescript car. The side door opened, and a man in sunglasses and a business suit covered by a black overcoat stepped out and looked with anticipation in Lee's direction. Lee shook his head, muttering, "I wonder who dresses these guys."

"Please," said the man in black, pointing to the open car door. Lee nodded and plopped down into the soft leather seats, sliding across to make room for his handler.

The door closed. The car was in motion. Lee looked around, trying to get his bearings, but immediately realized that the privacy glass was coated on both sides. No one could see in, but no one in the back compartment could see out. Before Lee could speak, the man did.

"I'm sorry, Dr. Brazil, but it's a necessary part of maintaining our privacy and security. We'll only be a few minutes. Sit back. Enjoy the ride. Would you like something to drink? Oh, you no longer drink, do you?"

Lee said nothing. Neither did his handler, as the car moved through the streets of Paris toward the Cathedral of Notre Dame. Much of the Cathedral had to be rebuilt and renovated after the great fire of 2019. As they came up to it, Lee thought that it looked as imposing as it had many years before, when he had first visited Paris. When the car stopped, the man cautiously opened the door and stepped out. He motioned for Lee and pointed to a side door of the cathedral. Lee followed his direction. The door opened as he approached it and slammed shut behind him after he entered.

The hallway was dark, the air cold and damp. It smelled of mold. At first, he couldn't see who had opened the door. But he sensed a presence just a few feet away. Lee stood still and stared into the dark until the outline of a man in a Monk's robe became clear. The figure silently pointed to another door about eighty feet away. Lee nodded and walked toward it. The figure didn't move from his post.

As he got closer to the large wooden door, Lee could hear the sound of a crowd. Holiday worshippers. Tourists who had come to see the great cathedral. Construction had begun in the twelfth century but wasn't completed until the fourteenth. The church had been desecrated during the French Revolution but survived to sound its bells on August 24, 1944, to announce to Parisians that the city had been freed from Nazi occupation.

With some difficulty, Lee cracked the door and peered into the great hall. He stepped through; closed the door; and, as instructed, lost himself in the crowd, which was quite easy to do. He gazed up at the organ.

"A beautiful work of art itself," said the tour guide. "Remarkably, the organ had survived the fire. Seventy-eight hundred pipes." Just as he thought of a question to ask the tour guide, a firm hand on his arm moved him toward a set of stairs that led to the vaults below. An attendant quickly removed the chain blocking the stairway. Lee and, he assumed, Andy proceeded down the stairs. At the bottom, Lee turned around.

Andy tried to speak first. "Dr. Brazil . . ."

But Lee interrupted him. "I'm tired of playing this stupid game. Here's your package." He reached into his breast pocket and pulled out the CD.

"No, no," said Andy. "Not here. You don't understand." "Well, I think I do," said Lee, his voice rising.

"You don't," said Andy with a firmness that got Lee's attention. "Your life is in danger. All our lives are in danger. That's why we changed . . ." his voice cracked, and he appeared quite distracted, "your mission."

Lee felt like saying that his only mission was to get home by Christmas in one piece. But he didn't.

Appearing to read his mind, Andy said, "We'd like to see that you get home safe. But first, you must deliver this package. It's not safe with me. *You* must get back to the States, to Boston, to Jennings. We have to get you out of Paris this afternoon."

"What the hell is on this damn . . . never mind. I don't want to know."

"Good," said Andy. "We have you booked on a charter flight to Bermuda this afternoon."

"Bermuda! Why Bermuda?"

Andy hesitated. "Well . . . it's um . . . a roundabout way of getting you back to Boston." Lee waited, but Andy said nothing else.

"Well, it's at least in the right direction."

"Exactly," said Andy.

"My lord, you're starting to sound like Jennings."

"Our man will meet your plane and make arrangements to get you off the island and back to Boston." Andy looked over his shoulder and called out, "Aman?"

93

A man stepped out of the dark and took Lee's arm. Lee shook his hand off, his anger once again flashing. "I may be getting old, but I've still got most of my teeth, and I can walk on my own."

Andy nodded and the man led Lee toward an exit door. "Watch your step," said Aman. "We must hurry. Your flight leaves at two-thirty."

Lee looked at his watch. "You've got to be kidding. It's after one. With security, we'll never make it." "Relax, we *are* security," said Aman.

"Right this minute, you'd have a hard time convincing me of that," said Lee. He was feeling pretty insecure at the moment.

Aman smiled.

"And what's happening with Liz? What am I going to tell her?" "Don't worry, Dr. Brazil," Aman responded. "We'll take care of all of that. We'll contact her through Qmail and explain that you've been delayed but will be arriving in Boston on the 24th." Lee didn't feel reassured.

"Well, you'd better do a good job of explaining why. What exactly are you going to tell her?"

"We must go," Aman said sternly and moved Lee toward the door.

CHAPTER 18

Cathedral of Notre Dame
Paris, France
Tuesday, December 21st, 1:35 P.M.

> *Well I've been to London and I've been to gay*
> *Paree . . .It's not dark yet, but it's getting there.*

~ Bob Dylan

The same limo was waiting at a different side entrance. Lee's previous handler opened the door and Lee slid across the seat. Aman took the seat next to the driver.

Bermuda, Lee thought. He hadn't been in Bermuda since he'd taken a cruise there with his family and his ninety-five-year-old mother. They'd gone mainly for her. She'd always wanted to go on a cruise. She'd loved it. It was her first and last. She died in the early winter of that year.

But there was something else about Bermuda. What was it? It took him a minute. Yes! Frank often traveled there. The patient with the strange dreams, who had disappeared then reappeared just before Lee had left. When Lee had checked in with his office yesterday, Loretta told him that Frank hadn't called back. The more Lee thought about it, Bermuda felt, in some strange way, like the right place to be going.

The limo drove through a security checkpoint and onto the tarmac. It stopped at the foot of the stairway usually reserved for loading food and supplies.

"We're here," said Aman. "Up the stairs now. Debbie will get you settled."

Lee objected. "Shouldn't we go around to the other side of the plane to board with the rest of the passengers?"

"That won't be necessary," said Aman, directing Lee toward the steps. "Off you go. Your luggage will be on a later flight." Lee hesitated.

"Don't look so concerned. Just enjoy the flight and look for our man when you get to Bermuda. He'll meet you."

Lee trudged up the steps, muttering, "Enjoy the ride. Enjoy the flight." When he reached the top, a young, blonde flight attendant was apparently waiting for him. "Mr. Jones," said Debbie.

Lee stepped through the cabin door. "I guess," he said, with obvious hesitation.

"Let me help you find your seat." She put her arm around Lee's waist from behind and walked him through the galley. She said something else that Lee couldn't make out. He could barely hear over the noise in the cabin. A drunken *Jingle-Bells* was competing for the attention of the group with an obscene version of *Frosty the Snowman*.

"Great," Lee grumbled, "a party plane."

"Yes," said Debbie, "but they should settle once we're in the air."

"Sure," he responded sarcastically.

"Here," said Debbie. "You're sitting next to Dr. Wagner."

A large man, slightly balding with white hair and large dark-rimmed glasses, Dr. Wagner appeared half in the bag, like most of the passengers. He rose and extended his hand as Debbie introduced them. Lee took his hand and tried to smile.

"Jones, eh?" he said. "You and half the people on this flight."

Lee looked puzzled. Wagner shook his head and smiled. "You don't understand, do you?"

Lee started to answer, but Wagner interrupted. "Most of the people on this flight work for the 'United States government.'" He gestured quotes with both hands, spilling some of his drink on the passenger in front of him.

Lee still didn't respond.

"It's a spook flight."

Lee's confusion deepened, and Wagner laughed loudly.

Wagner leaned over and whispered, or attempted to whisper, "CIA."

Lee smiled. "I see."

"Everyone needs a little R&R around the holidays, even," he leaned closer to Lee again, "spies. Right?"

"Right," Lee agreed.

The pilot interrupted their conversation to announce that the plane would be taxiing out for takeoff and that everyone should please take their seats and buckle in.

The flight attendants were busy handing out last call before takeoff and trying to herd passengers into their seats. The noise level increased as the pilot maneuvered the plane into position for takeoff and passengers shouted to be heard.

Dr. Wagner was having difficulty finding his seatbelt buckle. Lee came to his assistance and snapped it in place,

"Thank you, good sir. Let me buy you a drink. Debbie?"

"No, that's quite all right. When we get in the air, you can buy me one," said Lee.

"O-k-ay," said Dr. Wagner, slurring the word.

The pilot advanced the engine throttle and the plane rumbled into the sky. Wagner ordered himself another drink and asked Lee what he would have.

"What the hell," said Lee, "A Jack Daniel's Manhattan." Debbie smiled. "Right away."

"So, why are you on this flight, Mr. Jones? What business do you have in Bermuda?"

Lee hesitated. "Well . . ."

"Come, come," said Wagner, "you can tell the good doctor. That's my job, to listen. I've listened to . . . well, you wouldn't believe what I've listened to."

Want to bet, Lee thought.

He waited and then continued. "Do you have a good story?" He looked at Lee and smiled. "Something more than just cheating on your wife or killing someone?" He looked away. "I've heard it all." He turned to Lee again. "How about sex with your pet . . . no, no?" He turned away again. "I've heard that one…was it a Golden Retriever or a Great Dane . . . I don't remember."

"Hey, haven't all clinicians?" Lee smiled. He remembered. It was a Great Dane, and he'd thrown up after the session.

"I could tell you stories about some of the people on this plane, but…" He put his finger over his mouth. "Mum's the word. Patient confidentiality, you know."

Lee knew. "I'm sure," he said, fumbling with the seat pocket, looking for the in-flight magazine. Wagner was making him very uncomfortable. Lee had tried to put aside much of the craziness that he'd dealt with in the past. But Wagner was pulling it up.

The man rambled on. "Most of them won't even speak to me in public. They pretend they don't know me when they run into me." He turned again to Lee. "Hell, we all work in the same building!" He finished his drink. "Drop their dirty laundry off with me then pretend they don't even know me." He leaned over Lee who now had his head buried in the in- flight magazine. "I hold their hands for months or, for a few years, and they don't know me. And the rest? They're scared of me," he sneered. "Afraid to even sit next to me on this plane."

Lee looked up, "Is that so?" But he knew it was so. That was one of the hardest parts of the job. He was the repository for other people's stuff, which often left little room for his own. That's what burnout was all about. Becoming cynical and angry.

The drinks came. After just a couple of sips, Lee was ready to cheer the good doctor on. He'd certainly been in the same place. In many ways, he'd felt the same and almost said so. But he didn't.

"So that's why I'm getting the hell out of the agency. Too many years. Too many sad stories. I'm full up." Wagner leaned back in his seat and closed his eyes. "I can't hold any more of other people's garbage. They can get themselves another shrink. I'm out of here January first."

He sat up and looked Lee in the eyes. "You know what I mean, don't you?"

Lee didn't respond. He certainly could have. He had as many stories to tell. Lee remembered how he'd felt when he first started in the business. He was going to change the world, just like the young police applicants he used to evaluate. Not as a cop, but as a psychologist. But, just like the young cops, he'd grown more cynical with every year.

Wagner continued to look at him again and forced Lee to make eye contact. "I think you do understand. Yes, I think you do." Wagner paused then his eyes widened. "Oh, shit, you're not from the front office, are you?" "No, no," said Lee. "I'm not. What you said will stay with me. Mum's the word."

"Good," said Wagner. He leaned back in his seat and closed his eyes. In a few minutes he was snoring.

Lee looked out the cabin window but could see nothing. He thought again about the toll that human misery had taken on him, on all those who try to alleviate it: healthcare providers, clergy, police officers, social workers, and folks in Lee's profession, like Wagner.

CHAPTER 19

Bermuda Air Space
Tuesday, December 21st, 6:38 P.M.

Cynicism: Idealism gone sour.

~ Will Herberg

L ee awakened to the pilot announcing that passengers should take their seats and check their seatbelts: there was turbulence up ahead, and the landing at Bermuda might not be perfect. Lee rubbed his eyes and pulled his seatbelt tighter. Dr. Wagner stirred briefly then resumed snoring. A number of people were in the aisle, arguing with the attendants about the need to take their seats, when the plane hit the first patch of "bumpy air," as the pilot had called it.

Suddenly, the plane seemed to lose altitude. "Bumpy air," agreed the young man sitting across the aisle from Lee, as he opened the in-flight magazine. Lee nodded and checked his seatbelt again. A few people in the aisle moved toward their seats. The plane lunged up and then down. A woman talking to a friend lost her balance. Her friend caught her before she fell into the aisle. The flight attendant was on the intercom again.

"Please," she said, "please take your seats."

A few more tipsy passenger held onto seat backs, luggage compartments, and their fellow passengers to take their seats. People were still talking and laughing, but, before most could reach their seats, the plane began a free fall like the descent of a rollercoaster. Lee hated carnival rides. He felt his seatbelt dig into his waist as he was lifted off his seat. His heart pounded. He was trying to take deep breaths but couldn't. The plane heaved again, and his stomach felt like it was going to explode out of his mouth and nose. Conversation and laughter stopped.

The plane pitched to the left then began a forward plunge, like an elevator car whose cable had snapped. People screamed and gasped as anything and anyone not stowed or secured by a seatbelt became airborne and bounced off the ceiling, walls, and passengers.

Somehow, the pilots managed to regain control of the plane. The plunge to Earth slowed, and the plane righted. The air became calm again. The bright lights of Hamilton glittered in the distance. Tragedy averted; the CIA's best and brightest from the French office would spy another day.

Unfortunately, the turbulence, combined with a considerable amount of alcohol and party food, had negatively impacted the digestive tract of most of the passengers. The sickening odor of vomit began to fill the plane. When they reached the gate, Lee and a most of the other passengers were immediately on their feet and ready to exit

As Lee made his way past the galley, someone call his name. Not Jones, Smith, or whatever it was supposed to be for "security," but Brazil. A large black man was standing at the end of the galley, next to the cabin door through which crewmen were now loading food and drink. He smiled and motioned for Lee to join him. Lee mouthed, "Me?" and the man nodded. Lee wasn't sure. He looked around for a member of the crew—to ask what, he wasn't sure. But they were busy helping others to their feet, icing bumped heads, and finding bags and suitcases that the owners, in an alcoholic fog, couldn't remember stowing into which compartment.

The man motioned again for Lee and, as if propelled by some sort of invisible force, Lee stepped over boxes of snack food and assorted liquor and beer to reach the crew exit. Just as he started to speak, the man turned and started down the stairs. Lee followed without hesitation.

The sky was dark and the night air heavy but cool and smelled of the ocean. Lee took a couple of deep breaths. They reached the bottom of the stairs and moved quickly across the tarmac toward an old gray Lincoln Town Car parked on the edge of the runway. The man opened the driver's door and motioned Lee to the passenger side. Lee complied, taking a seat next to his guide.

"I take it you're the person who was sent to . . ."

The man nodded as he started the car, slipped it into gear, and headed toward the nearest exit gate. At this hour of the early evening, the small airport looked almost abandoned.

Lee continued, "You work for the Agency . . . I mean the United States government?"

"David," he said. "My name is David."

As they approached the gate, the guard opened it, smiled, and waved them through.

For a while, they followed a gravel road that ran parallel to the airport's runway. It soon turned into a narrow, newly paved road. The lights of the airport faded. It was pitch dark—no moon. It was only 7:00 or 7:30 Bermuda time, but Lee's biological clock told him that it was the wee hours of the morning European time and that he should be asleep. He was having difficulty keeping his eyes open. Lee shook himself and rubbed his eyes. "Where are we?"

"St. Georges."

"More importantly, where the hell are we going?"

"Not far," said David. "Twenty-five miles is a short commute in the United States. In Bermuda, it's the length of our country."

"You're from Bermuda?" asked Lee.

"I am now," David said with obvious pride. "I came here many years ago. It's a long story that I'll tell you tomorrow."

"Okay," said Lee with hesitation. "That's something I need to know?"

"You'll understand when I tell you. But tonight, we rest. Tomorrow, we talk."

They turned off the paved road onto sand and broken pavement.

Lee could hear the ocean. The headlights reflected off piles of debris, rotting buildings, and aging concrete bunkers. An old military base, Lee thought.

"Let me try again. Where are you taking me?" This time he asked with some force.

"I told you, we will be there in a few minutes." Lee started to object, then thought better of it.

David drove into a driveway that ran on an incline to a large concrete structure. He pulled the car up to two large, rusted metal "blast" doors.

"Dr. Brazil, please open the glove box and hand me the garage door opener."

Lee complied, retrieving a large, gray metal object that looked to him like a Buck Rogers ray gun. He handed it to David, who pointed it at a spot on the left door. Both doors began to slide silently back. As David pulled into the bunker, the doors closed behind them.

"That's one heck of a garage door opener," observed Lee.

David smiled. "We'll spend the night here." He slipped out of the car, and Lee followed him into a dimly lit room filled with electronic equipment—some vintage World War II, others high tech. So high tech that Lee didn't recognize it, though he knew a bit about electronics. He looked for a corporation label or serial number but saw none.

"Your bed is over there," David motioned, "and there's food in the kitchenette if you're hungry."

Lee was still looking at the room and equipment.

"The bath is in that corner," David said, pointing. "Did you hear me?"

"Ah . . . yes. What is all this? Where's the deluxe room on the beach? What's with the *I Spy* bunker?" asked Lee, looking perplexed.

"We've been planning for your arrival for some time," said David.

"My arrival?" echoed Lee with concern.

"We're here, because infrared scanners cannot detect our presence."

"You lost me on that one. Whose infrared scanners?"

"For tonight, just let me say, Dr. Brazil, that if the party who was supposed to meet you at the airport had, you would be dead by now. So, enjoy your good fortune. We'll talk in the morning. There are towels and clean clothes on your bed. I have work to do before tomorrow, so if you'll excuse me . . ."

Lee stood for a few seconds, while David, appearing not to notice, busied himself at one of the *Star Wars Galactica* control panels.

He decided to take David's advice and washed his face, noting deep, dark circles under his eyes. As his father would have said, "You look like hell warmed over." Less than a day ago, he'd been sitting in a hotel room in France. Now he was in a World War II era bunker in Bermuda with some guy who said that he'd saved his life, so he should be grateful.

He was too tired to give all this more thought, at least tonight. He did think of Liz. She'd be worried; he hadn't talked with her for a day. He'd left his cell phone in Paris. Even if he had it, it wouldn't work inside a reinforced concrete bunker.

He sat on the bed and took off his shoes then checked to make sure that the package was still in the breast pocket of his coat. The *Greatest Hits of Rock 'n Roll, Volume I,* was still there. David had said nothing about the package. Maybe . . . no, David had to know about the package. That was the whole point of Lee being here.

He moved the "clean clothing" to the chair by his bed. The clothes looked like a workmen's uniform. The breast pocket boasted an insignia of a cruise ship. *The Saint,* the one that sailed out of Boston to Bermuda. Lee shook his head and closed his eyes.

CHAPTER 20

Office of Dick Chambers
Hollocore, Dallas, Texas
Tuesday, December 21st, 3:45 P.M.

Pessimist: One who builds dungeons in the air.

~ Walter Winchell

Dick Chambers was on the phone with Reggie Brown, head of security for Hollocore. "What do you mean, they put the courier on a plane to Bermuda? That wasn't the plan. Can't these guys get anything right?" Chambers paused.

"You what? You don't know where he is? Hell, Bermuda is a small Island! How could you have lost track of him? Chambers stood up.

"You lost track of him at Wade International? It's not LaGuardia, for Christ's sake! Find him, damn it, or you'll be working as a security guard at Wal-Mart!"

Chambers slammed down the phone and plopped into his desk chair, muttering about the fools who worked for him. He hit the intercom button. "Shirley, get Special Agent Douglas Jennings on the phone."

A minute later, the phone buzzed. He picked up the receiver . . . "What do you mean, don't call you at this number? I'll call you at any number that I want. I have your director's cell phone number. James and I are planning on having dinner the next time I'm in DC. Would you like for me to call him? . . . Okay, then. Tell me what's going on with Brazil. Brown lost track of him . . . I know he's in Bermuda, but where? . . . And why the hell is he in Bermuda? . . . I thought you told me this fellow would do what he was supposed to do. Wouldn't be any trouble . . . I know all of that. And why, in the name of Mike, did your man in Paris put him on a CIA flight to Bermuda with agents from the Paris office?" Chambers' voice was rising. "Aren't these the same bozos who lost a laptop with the identification and facial-recognition data on every courier our government has or had used in the last twenty years? . . . Why didn't you guys just paint a bulls-eye on his back and announce on the public address system that he's on a mission for the U.S. Government? . . . Look, I don't want any more excuses or screw- ups. Find him, unless you want to retire from the Bureau early."

He slammed the phone down a second time. "I shouldn't have allowed those idiots to handle something this important." He walked over to the windows and looked out on the city. Another cloudy day. It looked like it might rain. Putting his right hand in his pocket, he fondled his good-luck piece then looked at his Rolex. He had to hurry or he might be late for his next meeting, and he didn't like being late.

Hamilton, Bermuda
Same Day, 7:45 P.M.

> *If you lose hope, somehow you lose that vitality that*
> *keeps life moving, you lose that courage to be, that*
> *quality that helps you to go on in spite of it all.*

~ Dr. Martin Luther King (1967)

TransSea had arranged a reservation for Jeff at a relatively nice hotel near their offices in Hamilton. He could walk there, and would. He'd arrived at Wade International late that afternoon, had a sandwich at the airport, and had gone directly to the hotel to check in.

As he began to walk toward the offices of TransSea, his excitement grew over the possibility of again having a well-paying job, but so did his confusion as to why he was to meet TransSea's representative at such a late hour, 9:00 P.M. Most shops and businesses had closed hours before. The section of Front Street housing TransSea appeared abandoned for the night.

The building, a bright, metallic blue TransSea embedded in a sea of stars, was easy to find, even in the dark. There was a security guard at the front desk who took Jeff's name, looked at his passport, and told him he wouldn't need to sign in. Mr. Perkins was expecting him.

"Fifth floor." He pointed to the elevator.

Jeff crossed the small lobby as the guard watched. He pushed the elevator button and noticed that his heart was pounding and he was perspiring, even though it was a relatively cool evening. He looked down at his shoes, thinking, I should have worn the other pair. The door opened on the fifth floor. The reception desk was empty. He stepped off the elevator.

"Jefferson..."

Jeff looked in the direction of the voice. "Yes?" He could see a person standing in the dimly lit hallway to his left. The figure motioned for him to follow, and Jeff complied.

Halfway down the hall, the figure turned into a small office, with a couple of chairs and a small desk. No papers, books, or pictures or electronic devices of any kind.

The figure turned to face him—a man in his late thirties, well-dressed in a gray business suit and tie. Jeff was wearing a clean shirt and jeans; the blazer dated back to high school, the one he'd worn to senior prom. There had been no money in the last few years for what his mother would call "dress-up clothes." His family had only been able to afford the basics.

"Please, sit down. I am Philip Perkins." He smiled. He had a soft voice.

He remained standing.

"Thank you," said Jeff, his voice cracking as it usually did when he was nervous. He sat down.

"I would offer you coffee, but everyone is gone for the day, and even I will not drink the coffee that I make." Jeff assured him that he would be fine without coffee. "Your flight and hotel?"

"Oh, very . . . very fine, sir." Jeff smiled again.

"I think that we are here to discuss a job," said Perkins. "In fact, two jobs. The first will require a few days of your time and some travel." He walked to the office window and looked out. "And the second, a permanent, well-paying job at our offices in Dallas, will be available to you if you do the first job to our satisfaction."

Jeff smiled a third time. He had a toothsome smile. "I'm certainly interested in both jobs. Things have been a little tight for us over the past few years. I want to get back to work."

"I am glad to hear of your interest. You were trained as a seaman by the U.S. Navy?"

Jeff nodded.

"And even tried out for the Seals, but, unfortunately, were not selected." Perkins' tone was more a statement than a question.

Jeff looked at the floor. Perkins continued to stare out the window.

"Yeah, that's why I didn't reenlist." "Yes, I know," said Perkins.

"So, what about the job—or jobs?" asked Jeff, trying not to show the old anger he still felt for the Navy.

"Well, Jefferson, let us focus on just the first job. As you know, TransSea has a close relationship with our military, especially the Navy. An informational package critical to our country has been taken from our government, which has lost track of both it and the individual who took it. We know that he is here in Bermuda and may be traveling to Boston in the next few days on a cruise ship." He paused and turned to face Jeff. "We have arranged for you to join the crew of that ship here in Bermuda. You must locate this individual and take the package from him before the ship docks in Boston on Christmas Eve."

"So, I have to find this guy by Christmas Eve?" Jeff tried to make eye contact with Perkins, but failed.

"Yes. We know that his female accomplice is an American crewmember."

"So, when I locate this guy, I take the package from him . . . without killing him."

"Yes. We would prefer it that way." Perkins placed a package wrapped in brown paper on the desk. "Our security people thought that this might come in handy." He handed Jeff the small package. "I think you are familiar with this device's operation."

Jeff looked at the package.

"It's a tranquilizer dart gun," said Perkins.

Jeff nodded.

"If you decide not to work with us, just toss it in a waste bin before you board your plane for home."

"And I have to get the package without him knowing who I am?"

"Yes, that is critical. Again, you must deliver the package to our office in Boston no later than midnight on Christmas Eve."

The conversation paused, then Perkins sat forward. "We will pay you ten thousand dollars for your trouble . . . up front. We will wire the money to your wife when you set sail."

Jeff started to speak, but Perkins cut him off.

"If you succeed, we will provide you with another fifteen thousand dollars in cash and a permanent job in the New Year. Think it over tonight, and email your decision to this account by 8:00 A.M. tomorrow." He handed Jeff a slip of paper. "*The Saint* docks tomorrow afternoon. Be on board the ship by 4:00 P.M. The chief steward, Ron Wilson, is expecting you. Any other questions?"

Jeff had none. Perkins showed him to the elevator.

He walked back to the hotel and called his wife. He hoped that he was making the right decision but didn't feel like he had much choice. He told Judy to expect a large signing bonus by wire and said that he would be home in a few days. She'd have to explain to the kids that he wouldn't be home for Christmas, given the limited holiday flights. Judy continued to sound suspicious of the whole affair. He knew that she had questions, but she didn't ask them, True to her word, she would go with his judgment.

Jeff didn't sleep well that night. He was up early, had coffee and a scone, and emailed Perkins the word "Yes" at 7:30. He went back to his room and tried to sleep but couldn't, so he checked out of the hotel at 1:00 and took a taxi to King's Wharf. *The Saint* had docked and was taking on fuel and supplies. He was welcomed aboard by Wilson, who explained his duties, gave him a quick tour of the ship, and assigned him a cabin on Deck 2. He walked around the ship, waiting for the employee cafeteria to open. He was hungry. While he waited, he stared out at the Atlantic and thought about what he had just signed on for.

He'd never killed a man. Not even in Afghanistan. He had hunted all his life and was an excellent shot, but he wasn't going to kill this man. If he did, it would be an accident. He was just going to take something and return it to the rightful owner. He was doing the right thing. Jeff was a man who always tried to do the right thing.

Cabin of Joann Lawrence
The Saint
North Atlantic Ocean
Wednesday, December 22nd, 3:23 A.M.

Joann couldn't sleep; she was full of energy. She'd had another strange dream; she couldn't remember it but awakened frightened. She heard voices through the door from the adjoining cabin, occupied by anothe crewman, Emanuel. They'd only exchanged greetings; she knew nothing of him.

Her room was filled with a bright blue light that she assumed was the moon shining through a sudden fog that had arisen. She was afraid to look out the porthole. She was drawn to the voices and went to the door to the adjoining room to listen, but the voices stopped.

She heard the cabin door to the hall open and close. She went back to bed but still couldn't sleep.

Morning finally came. She was first in line for breakfast in the employee cafeteria.

CHAPTER 21

Kings Wharf, Bermuda
December 22, 2027, 7:20 A.M.

*All things work out in the end and if
they have not, it is not the end.*

~ Old Saying from India

The driver opened the door, and Joann smiled and took a seat in the back of the taxi. "St. Paul's," she said.

The church was on the other end of the island, at least forty-five minutes away. Joann was carrying a small gold cross that her grandfather had given to her. He had served at St. Paul's as a young priest. She'd decided just a couple of weeks ago to return the cross to the church. She still wasn't completely sure why. She'd just begun to feel that she should, which was strange, because she seldom made decisions based only on her feelings.

The winter sun felt warm on her skin. She closed her eyes and drank it in. She was tired. She hadn't slept well on the ship. On her first night onboard *The Saint,* the sea had been rough, and last night . . . last night she had been awakened by . . . well, she wasn't sure what had disrupted her sleep. When she'd awakened, her entire body seemed filled with some kind of energy. She tossed and turned. Her thoughts raced. Her heart pounded. She'd been up for the rest of the night.

And this morning, she was once again filled with emotion. Her thoughts went back to a December many years ago, when the Great Recession had forced her to close her store. She remembered that afternoon well. It was cold and gray. Night was falling. She hated the dark, and it came on early. The forecast was rain, but it looked like snow to her. She closed early on holidays. It was the last day of the year. Why she'd bothered to open, she wasn't completely sure. For thirty years, she'd always opened on New Year's Eve. She guessed she wanted today to be no different. But it would be.

Business was expectedly slow. By New Year's Day, people had had their fill of children's books and toys. But that had always been okay. So what if the last week of the year was slow? November and December sales had always been strong and carried her through, at least in the past. The holidays brought people to the Old City. By New Year's Eve, she could sigh with relief, having survived another year. And that's what it had felt like the last few years. This year, like the two before, hadn't been good. Oh, the Old City had been filled with people like it always had, but they'd bought less and were searching for something different. They weren't looking for toys or books for their children. They were looking to forget that these, like so many things, were items that they could no longer afford. So, they didn't come into her shop. They went to the bars to forget about the jobs they didn't have or the mortgage payments they couldn't make.

She'd told herself that things would get better. She had hoped. She had prayed. They hadn't. But she'd pulled through hard times before, other recessions in '01 and '08. This wasn't the first she'd weathered. But each one had taken a bit more out of her, both emotionally and financially, and those bits hadn't returned since the "recovery." Neither had her savings, which were gone. The previous month, she'd sold the last piece of stock she had left after the crash, the last of her inheritance from her mother. who had died twelve years before.

Her attorney had told her to close the store before the New Year. She'd just spoken with him that morning. A nice man, competent, and he gave good advice, she was sure, but he didn't understand. The store had been her life, her dream. She'd done it, lived it, breathed it, loved it. Few people really understood how important it was to her. Her sister had understood and so had Lee. They'd been together when she'd opened it. But she'd focused on her shop and he on his career, and they'd eventually gone their own ways. He'd married. She hadn't.

But life is strange, she thought. She'd gotten a Christmas card from him just the week before. Strange indeed. She hadn't heard from him in years. He'd asked how she was. She had replied immediately with a New Year's card that wished him well and said that all was fine with her. But it wasn't. How did he know? Or did he? She thought back to the life they'd had before the shop.

Loud voices from the street outside filtered through the windows. She shook her head. This wasn't the time to think about the past. She had things to do before she . . . closed.

Her shop was empty. The last customer had left an hour earlier. She walked toward the door but hesitated. She should close now, before some drunk came in, saying that he was looking for a book for his kids. They usually never bought anything. They were just lonely and wanted company. Someone to talk to. She hadn't minded in the past, but tonight—tonight *was* different.

She opened the front door, took down the "Open" flag, pulled in the sandwich board, and locked the door. She straightened up the shelves, put away the day's receipts, flipped on the vacuum, and moved down the middle aisle. Her eyes began to fill. She turned off the vacuum. She would finish it tomorrow. She would do the inventory tomorrow. She would finish it all tomorrow.

She put on her coat, tied her scarf tightly around her neck, and took one last look at her shop. The tears came again. She picked up her purse, turned off the light, and closed the door, stepping onto Market Street.

The wind off the bay was strong and cold. It was starting to snow.

Joann could remember it all as if it were yesterday. She remembered that horrible winter. The cold and snow. She followed her attorney's advice and gave the keys to the bank. She went home and sat in front of the television as if paralyzed. Some days, she forgot to eat. She applied for jobs, but there were no jobs. She filed for bankruptcy.

She looked out the taxi window. She'd lost track of where they were. They'd already passed Hamilton. She tried to focus on the present. Things did get better. Summer finally came. She finally found another job. Things turned around.

She leaned back again and closed her eyes, returning to her memories, recalling the Friday afternoon when she'd bought the lottery ticket. She never won anything. She didn't consider herself a lucky person. But she'd felt like doing something different that afternoon. The same feeling she now had about returning the gold cross. So, she'd bought the ticket.

The drawing was the next night. She tuned in to watch the news and barely paid attention when they began to announce the winning numbers. But amazingly, her numbers came up. She became a millionaire. She finally came into money.

The taxi stopped. The driver got out and opened the door. Joann didn't move.

"Miss?"

Joann began to fumble with her purse for the fare. She stepped out of the taxi and gave the driver a large tip.

"Thank you," he said twice.

She looked up at the tower and the clock and started up the steps to St. Paul's.

CHAPTER 22

Abandoned Military Base
St. Georges, Bermuda
Wednesday, December 22nd, 7:30 A.M.

I call to remembrance my song in the night.

~ Psalms

L ee woke numerous times in the night, confused as to where he was. At one point, he was convinced that he was still on the plane bound for Bermuda, that he had fallen asleep, as Dr. Wagner droned on about his ungrateful patients and the "agency." Finally, exhaustion had its way, and he fell into a deep sleep.

He woke early. At least he thought it was early; by his internal clock it was. His head was filled with the words from a hymn. "Draw the circle wider, draw it wider still . . . no one stands alone."

Lee lay back and tried to remember the dream he'd had. It came to him very clearly. It was about his old friend Griff, who had hired him and brought him to Maine so many years ago. Griff became a lifelong friend. He'd encouraged Lee and Liz to adopt. He'd been there for Lee when he returned from detention in Boston. He was one of the few people Lee had confided in about his problems with alcohol.

In the dream, Griff was trying to tell Lee something. From the expression on his face, it must have been something important. Lee could understand the words, "You must understand," but the rest was drowned out by static, the kind you'd hear on an old television.

He hadn't seen Griff for about three years. No one had. Griff had taken his lobster yacht, as he called it, on a trip down the coast and had disappeared somewhere near Cape Hatteras. Authorities had never found his body or any wreckage from the boat. Lee sighed and took a deep breath. It was nice having him back, even if only in a dream.

Lee tried to look around the room, but it was dark. And cold. He fumbled for his watch, the one his daughter had given him. He found it but couldn't read it. The only light came from the configuration of lights and symbols on the display panels that Lee had watched David manipulate last night until he could no longer hold his eyes open. Lee folded back the blanket and slowly swung his legs around to the edge of the bed. He rubbed his eyes, placed his feet quietly on the concrete floor and stood up. Suddenly, the room was flooded with light. David appeared in the door at the end of the room, the one leading into the garage.

"Oh, you're awake. It's getting late. We really must go." "Go where?" asked Lee.

"To visit an old friend of mine. But first, we eat. Would you like some eggs and bacon? Scrambled, I'm afraid. Government issue."

"Well, coffee is what I'd really like. A lot of it," said Lee.

"We have that. Come." He motioned Lee to a table near the door. "Cream and sugar?"

"Just cream. I think I'll pass on the eggs. I've had government issue before." Lee didn't say when and where, but it had been in the detention center. Lee felt the cold come over him and tried to shake it off.

"Just coffee, then?" asked David.

Lee nodded and sat down at the table. David poured and he stirred. He took a few sips of the coffee, which must not have been Government Issue, because it didn't taste like dishwater.

"Now, let me look at you," said David. He was holding a screen in his hand that displayed a 3-D image of a man who had a similar build and facial features to Lee. "No, no," he said with a grimace. "We must do something about your hair—or I should say lack of it.

And the skin tone. Of course, this tone isn't right."

Once again, Lee was taken aback. "What are you talking about?"

David ignored his question and continued his inspection. "Hmm, height and build are okay. Maybe a few pounds over, but it'll work." He stopped. "Well, I guess we'll just have to let Edward . . ."

"Let Edward do what?" asked Lee anxiously.

"Match you with Emanuel, so you can get back to Boston."

"Why are we 'matching' me with anyone? Does this guy Emanuel have a prosthetic hook where a left hand should be?"

David didn't answer.

Lee paused and thought for a moment. "Okay. That sounds okay, especially the part about getting back to Boston. So, where's the toupee and make-up?"

"Oh, we won't need those. Just get dressed. We need to leave before the fog burns off."

Lee splashed water onto his face, quickly dressed, and drained his coffee cup. He was ready for Edward or Emanuel, or whatever he was ready for. He wasn't quite sure.

"Turn around," said David.

Lee complied, and David carefully examined the uniform he had provided for Lee the night before. "A good fit," he observed. "Now, for

Edward. It's time."

"Okay," said Lee, looking around, puzzled. "And who . . . where . . . is Edward?"

"He's right . . ."

". . . here," said a voice from behind Lee. "David failed to introduce us last night. You were so tired."

"Yes, I was," said Lee, turning in the direction of the voice and looking more confused.

"Dr. Brazil," said David, "let me introduce my assistant, Edward Zan." Lee continued to scan the room.

"I am standing in front of you, Dr. Brazil."

118

"You—you're a computer?"

"I am what your race might call strong artificial intelligence, a label equally insulting and not an accurate description of who I really am."

Thank God his name isn't Hal, Lee thought, remembering *2001: A Space Odyssey.*

"I'm sorry, Edward. I'm afraid I've never met a . . . a . . . ."

"Another life form like me," Edward finished for him.

Lee recalled that when the human crew tried to disconnect Hal, he killed most of them.

"Yes," said Lee, fumbling for words, "another life form like you."

"I could materialize into a life form like yourself, if you would be more comfortable."

"Yes . . . I . . . no. Oh, no. That won't be necessary," floundered Lee. Materialize, he thought. What the hell is he talking about? "You mean like a holographic image?"

"Yes, that is what you humans call it. Very crude. I can create, as you would say, 'the real McCoy.'"

"Edward," David interrupted, "we must leave in the next few minutes."

"Yes. I suppose that there is no time to talk now. Okay. Dr. Brazil, please sit down and face me." Lee complied at first then stood back up. "Now, wait a minute. What are you going to do to me?"

"To put it in layman terms, I am going to stimulate your hair follicles in such a way that your hair will grow very rapidly. Then I'm going to remove a few wrinkles and give you a suntan. All perfectly safe."

Lee still looked skeptical.

"These are very simple procedures," said Edward. "Your race will master this process in a few years. Please sit down and face me. We have no more time."

Lee sat back down but continued to object. "I'm not sure about . . ." Before he could say more, he felt a warm sensation spread across his face and his head. His scalp tingled. It was over. "Oh, yes. Very nice. Would you agree, David?" "You're a genius, Edward," said David.

"Yes, I know," said Edward matter-of-factly.

Lee felt his face. No real change. But when he touched his forehead and scalp, he found much more hair than he'd had a few minutes before. He jumped from his seat and looked at his reflection in one of the screens. Yes, he had hair. It was gray and thin, but he looked years younger. And his face and hand had turned a light brown. Many of his wrinkles had disappeared. He looked at David with anticipation.

"We can talk about this later," said David. "We have no time. We must get to Sharks Hole before the fog is gone."

He shoved a fishing rod into Lee's hand. "I'll carry the tackle box and my rod."

"We're going fishing?" Lee was even more puzzled, if that were possible.

"We just need to look like we're going fishing. Now, come along, Emanuel. We only have a few hours before *The Saint* sails."

"I'm going to Boston on a ship?"

"Yes, it's necessary. Now we must go."

Lee followed David. The fog was thick, and the path to Sharks Hole difficult, even in full daylight. Lee used caution as he picked his way along the rocky slope leading to the beach. His head was still spinning.

"Hurry along, Dr. Brazil. I must insist. We're almost there."

The sun was starting to break through the fog as they reached the rocky outcropping that marked the entrance to the sea cave that was Sharks Hole.

CHAPTER 23

Shark's Hole
St. Georges, Bermuda
Wednesday, December 22nd, 8:35 A.M.

Out of the crooked timber of humanity,
no straight thing can be made.

~ Immanuel Kant

T he cave was cold, and the air was damp and smelled of the ocean. The narrow trail opened into a large room. As Lee's eyes adapted to the dark, it was clear that the ceiling of the cave was eighty to ninety feet from the rock-strewn floor. The large room opened onto the ocean on its north side. At high tide, Lee imagined that entering from the sea wouldn't be possible, even in a small boat.

"This way," David yelled over the roar of the water. "Here's a torch." He handed Lee a small flashlight. The two walked into the dark. In the back of the cave was an old boathouse, a very old boathouse that had likely seen many a storm.

David unlocked the padlock and pulled the chain away.

"Come help me with our transportation. Here, hold the torch while I open the doors. We'll slide her out and run her down the traces to the water."

The doors swung open and the light revealed a Boston Whaler.

"How old is the boathouse?" asked Lee.

"Well, it's younger than I am. I built it the first year I was on the island."

"It's got to be older than twenty or thirty years."

"Oh, it is. Here." He handed Lee the light. "There's something else I want you to see."

David walked to the back of the boathouse and unlocked another set of double-doors.

"Hand me the torch." He moved the light across the bow of a wooden boat much older than the Whaler. I was covered in dust, sand, and cobwebs that hadn't seen the sea for many years.

"This was my transportation to the island." David waited.

Lee said nothing.

"A lifeboat," said David.

"I don't know very much about these things, but it looks like a very old one."

"Yes, and a very special one." David's light fell on *Carol A. Deering.*

Lee squinted and moved closer, mouthing the name again. "No. No, I don't think so."

"You know the story, don't you? I assume that many people in Maine do. She was built in Bath for the Deering Company of Portland."

"Yes," Lee added, "in the 1920s."

David nodded and continued. "She was a fine schooner. She was returning from Rio in January of 1921, sailing light, no cargo, bound for Norfolk, Virginia. We'd last made port in Barbados."

"Storytellers call her a ghost ship," said Lee, and David nodded. "The Coast Guard found her grounded in Cape Hatteras in early February. The crew wasn't aboard. She'd been abandoned, and the captain's log and all her papers and instruments were gone, too." David nodded again. "Most ships run aground when they have no direction or crew," said Lee.

"That's correct," said David. "Ships are like people. With no direction, they become lost."

"They never found the crew or the lifeboats?" Lee asked.

"No, and no wreckage ever washed ashore," added David.

Lee looked at David again, unsure of where this was leading.

"You may not know, Dr. Brazil, but most of the crew consisted of Danes and Finns and . . ."

"One black man." Lee closed his eyes. "And I suppose you're that man."

David nodded again.

"That makes you a hundred and thirty years old." "A hundred and thirty-two, to be exact," said David.

Lee turned to face David. His face was bright red. "Enough," said Lee. "I can take a joke. I can deal with a smartass computer that does tricks, but you don't look . . ."

"My age," said David.

Lee took a breath. He touched to the boat, rubbing at the paint.

"Gently. She's an old girl. And as you can see, the paint isn't fresh. Do you want to hear the story of the *Carol A. Deering* that you don't know?"

"Yes, I suppose I do."

David pointed to an equipment bench, and the two sat down. "We have time now. Edward tells me that another fogbank is rolling in, so we should be fine."

David began: "The *Carol Deering* sailed light from Barbados on January the 9th, 1921. The weather was good, the wind strong. The days passed quickly and were uneventful. We sailed easily by the Cape Fear lightship off the coast of North Carolina on the 23rd. What happened next, I'll try to describe."

"I'm sure that will be hard, since you couldn't possibly have been there," said Lee with a smirk.

"Dr. Brazil, you said that you would hear me out."

Lee nodded, "Yes, I did. And I will. Continue."

"On the evening of the 24th, most crewmembers were in the main cabin. They'd just sat down for dinner. I was standing watch with the first mate. Captain Wormell was in his cabin. It was just after sunset. The sky was clear, the last light of day disappearing in the

West. The wind, which had been strong, suddenly died away. The water became still and calm, and we slowed to a stop. A strange quiet came over the ship and the sea. Then we saw it. Off starboard. A bright, metallic blue light. It got brighter and larger as it approached."

Lee crossed his arms and sighed.

"Something few know is that we had a passenger aboard, a young priest, Father Michael Lawrence."

Lee looked stunned, remembering his dream. "Yes."

"He was bound for Portland, Maine. What he was doing in Barbados. I don't know. I believe he had some connection to Captain Wormell." David paused, "I never learned of what kind. He was on deck when the light appeared. He seemed to be waiting for it."

It had been difficult, but David now had Lee's complete attention. What had happened in Winterpool just a couple of weeks before: His missing patient, the fire, the strange circular patterns in the grass, the melted car, and his obsessive dreams about the ships. But even more, Lee was remembering a time when he was sixteen, camping with friends. A light had approached the campsite. When Lee and his friends attempted to approach it, it quickly moved away. Over the next week, the light appeared numerous times. Just after sunset and just out of reach, it always moved away quickly when approached. It appeared for seven nights then disappeared and didn't return. "Are you listening, Dr. Brazil?"

Lee nodded, and David continued, "We watched the light without speaking. There seemed to be no reason to speak. I sensed that we weren't alone in the wheelhouse. I turned, and a young man I'd never seen before was standing behind us. He was blond, dressed as a seaman, but he wasn't a member of our crew. Without words, he asked us to follow him. To abandon the bridge. We complied."

Lee was now mesmerized by the story and could almost see the face of the young seaman in his dream with the bright green eyes.

"The crew had left the main cabin and were on deck, beginning to lower the ship's lifeboats. Captain Wormell was loading his charts and instruments and the ship's log into one. The young man, again without words, asked our first mate to assist him, so he did."

Lee interrupted, "What do you mean, without words? Why are you telling me all of this?"

"You'll understand later. I can't explain now." David continued, "We knew what he was asking and we knew that we should follow his direction."

"Jeez Louise," mumbled Lee, looking away.

"Father Michael was still standing near the bow, staring at the light. It hadn't moved. The young man asked me to follow him. He took Father Michael by the arm and led him to a lifeboat. We were the only ones left on the schooner. He handed Father Michael a small gold cross with seven green stones embedded in it. Then he told me to lower the boat into the water and join Father Michael. I did."

Lee said nothing.

"All the lifeboats were now away. Suddenly, a heavy fog rolled in from the west then from the east. One by one, it swallowed the lifeboats. The young man was still on deck, watching our departure, as the fog rolled over the *Carol Deering*. Neither he nor any of our crew had spoken a word."

Lee shook his head in disbelief. This *was* his dream.

"I could see nothing in the fog but the cross. The stones gave off a strange greenish light. It seemed to be directing the boat. I lit a lantern. We had a compass, but it was of no value; the needle just spun wildly. Father Michael and I took turns rowing." He paused. "But our efforts weren't what propelled us across the water. When daybreak came, we were just a few hundred yards from here." David shook his head and looked away. "I can't tell you how we had crossed so many miles of ocean in just a few hours."

"What happened to the rest of the crew?" questioned Lee.

"I don't know." David shook his head again. "Edward told me that they were safe and no harm came to them."

"The *Carol Deering* didn't run aground until early February. It was sighted two more times off the Carolina coast in late January," Lee stated.

"Yes, I know." David hesitated. "I have no idea what use they had for the ship or why they wanted the crew to abandon her." He seemed unsure of his next words: "They've never told me." "They? Who are they?" Lee's anger flashed.

"Someone you'll meet later this morning may have more answers. I don't know who they are. I didn't encounter them again until after the war, World War II. Father Allen told me they that they'd returned because of the atomic bombs that were dropped on Nagasaki and Hiroshima." He paused. "Apparently, our first steps into space were also alarming to them. Now they've returned again out of concern."

"Out of concern." Lee repeated. "Why now?"

"I'll let Father Allen explain. It was to his church—an Episcopal Church, old St. Paul's—that the cross led us that morning. The church helped me find work in Bermuda, and I helped Father Michael get to Maine. I married. My wife and I had two children." David sighed, "I've outlived all three of them. Life extension was their gift to me, and the cross was their gift to Father Michael."

"Wait a minute. This young man you mentioned, the one without words, that was Edward?" asked Lee.

"Yes. It was many years before I encountered him again, in the early Sixties." David again appeared unsure of his words. "I know it may sound strange, but Edward needed my assistance with another ship, *The Enchantress*, a yacht also built in Bath in the mid-1920s. A beautiful ship. Fifty-nine feet. Teak decks, mahogany trim. She fell on hard times. In the Fifties, a millionaire bought her at auction and refitted her." David began walking toward the bow of the whaler. Lee followed.

"On her maiden voyage, she ran into a gale off Florida. The Coast Guard couldn't reach the family—a father, mother, and two young boys—and the small crew in time. But they were saved."

Lee recalled the dream he'd had in London a few days earlier. "The official report was that the ship and all aboard were lost."

"No. They're safe."

They were silent for a time. Finally, Lee spoke, "Why did Edward the genius computer need your assistance?" His skepticism was back.

"I helped him disassemble the ship. My father was a shipbuilder. I learned the trade before going to sea. I actually knew a few things that Edward didn't! My last encounter with Edward is the present one." He motioned to Lee, "Help me get the boat into the water. We have to go."

David helped Lee into the boat and started the small outboard motor. The boat slipped out into the fog, toward the Village of St. Georges.

CHAPTER 24

A beach near St. Paul's
St. Georges, Bermuda
Wednesday, December 22nd, 8:40 A.M.

Reach high, for stars lie hidden in your soul. Dream
deep, for every dream precedes the goal.

~ Pamela Vaull Starr

F ather Allen was taking his morning walk. He was an average
man by most standards, perhaps a bit on the heavy side, who
looked to be in his late fifties. Graying black hair, casual dress:
slacks, Bermuda shirt, and sandals. The weather was clear but cool,
with some fog. He loved this time of day and being by himself. He
could think . . . and he had much to think about today. He understood
from his dream last night that late this morning, he would have a
visitor, a woman, who would return something to the church that
was lost many years ago, and that, if asked, she would assist him
with a second visitor whom he would receive later in the day.

They had been communicating with him in this way for many
years. It began when he took charge of St. Paul's. He didn't know
who authored the dreams, but he'd learned to pay attention to them
and follow their direction.

The dreams had told him months ago that his second visitor would
arrive today, accompanied by Father Allen's friend David, and that
he and David must keep the true identity of this visitor secret while
assisting him in obtaining safe passage to Boston.

Father Allen and David had arranged for him to assume the
identity of a crewman on *The Saint*, a cruise ship that would set sail

for Boston later that afternoon.

Father Allen picked up his pace. He had much to do before his visitors arrived.

Shark's Hole
St. Georges, Bermuda
Same Day, 9:15 A.M.

Pessimist: One who burns his bridges before he gets to them

~ Sidney Ascher

Lee sat in the bow of the boat. Through the fog, he could see no more than ten feet ahead. He said nothing, trusting that David, at least according to his story, was an old—very old—seaman and could handle the situation.

Lee put his focus on trying to understand, to believe, what he'd heard and seen in the last few hours. His previous trip to Europe that had included a delivery for Jennings had been relatively uneventful. He'd expected the same on this trip, not people trying to kill him, a side trip to Bermuda, or David and Edward and the story of the *Carol Deering.* And who were "They?" Little green men from Mars?

He wanted to believe that all this was some elaborate ruse. The lifeboat. That was the only hard piece of evidence, and it could be fake. And the talking computer? That wouldn't be difficult these days. But the new hair was real. Lee tugged at it. Rogaine has strong competition, he mused. A quick skin tanning? No problem for these guys. No sprays or tanning lights required So, what did he have? A lifeboat from a ghost ship, a talking computer, tall tales from a man who said that he was 132 years old, a super hair-replacement system, and some strange dreams. And the man Emanuel, who was now evidently his twin . . . almost. They'd forgotten one important detail: The hook. How many Emanuels were walking around with a prosthetic hook?

But for what purpose was all this? If they wanted the package, they could have taken it, but David had said nothing about it.

They were nearing the center of the bay, and the water was becoming choppy. The fog started to lift; St. Georges was coming into clear view. They would soon make shore. Lee scanned the horizon, trying to keep a small case of seasickness from becoming a large one. Focus on the horizon, he reminded himself.

To the west of St. Georges, he saw something in the sky. At first, he thought it was a plane from Wade International. As it grew closer, he could hear the chop, chop, chop of a helicopter. It was moving fast and heading directly for them, slowing as it neared. Within a few seconds, it was directly overhead and started to descend. The water around the boat became even rougher and washed over the gunnels. Lee caught a rope tie with his hook and clutched the right gunnel in a death grip. David increased their speed and began shouting and waving the helicopter off.

The boat could be swamped, Lee thought, but Boston Whalers never sink. At least that's what he remembered from reading one of those sailing magazines that his partner Bill used to bring to the office.

A rope ladder appeared from the side of the helicopter, unrolled, and dangled in the wind. A figure dressed in black, attached to the craft by a cable, began to descend. Lee's deep breathing was no longer working. Fear began to take control. Over the roar of the helicopter, Lee could hear David. "Don't worry, Dr. Brazil. They're going to have engine problems in just about . . . ten seconds."

As predicted, by the count of ten, its engines began to misfire, and black smoke poured from the exhaust. The pilot pulled the craft away and headed back, now moving slowly, in the direction from which they'd come.

The water calmed, and David slowed the boat. They were heading for a boathouse. As they approached, the large double doors opened then closed immediately behind them with a clang. The boathouse was dark and smelled of fish. One light hung from a rafter near the back. A man stood under it. He wore the same uniform as Lee. He reached out to help David moor the boat.

It was then that Lee noticed it: The hook for his left hand. He assisted Lee from the boat. David quickly introduced them. "Dr. Brazil, Emanuel Rodriguez. Emanuel, Dr. Brazil." They shook hands and nodded.

"A beautiful match," said David. "Even I would have difficulty telling you apart. But, enough, Emanuel and I must go. I'll find other transportation for him to Boston. But first we must deal with our good friends from Hollocore. I'm sure that they sent the helicopter. They would love to have the package you're carrying, Dr. Brazil."

"You know about the package?" asked Lee, surprised.

"Yes, of course."

"And what . . ."

"We haven't time to talk more," David interrupted, "our friends will be returning, and I assume that you don't want to meet them. If you believe what I've told you, go to St. Paul's. Father Allen is expecting you. He doesn't know about Edward and much of what I've told you about the *Carol Deering*. We . . . I mean, *I* would prefer to keep it that way. I've told him only that they've arranged a disguise for you. An old friend of yours is with Father Allen, awaiting you."

Lee opened his mouth to ask who, but closed it abruptly, knowing that David would only interrupt him again.

David glanced at his watch then looked intently at Lee. "You see, each of us is only a small piece of the puzzle. Mine is Edward and the *Carol Deering*. Now go, while you still can. You'll eventually understand what I've told you. But if you choose not to wait for understanding, take your chances in St. Georges. Unfortunately, I doubt that you'd last very long."

Emanuel opened the door that led up the dock into the street. Lee looked back at David.

"Good-bye, Dr. Brazil, and good luck," said David. "Yes, well . . . Thank you, David . . . and you, Emanuel." David smiled. Emanuel nodded.

"Thank you, I think," Lee said under his breath, as he started up the dock toward St. Paul's.

CHAPTER 25

St. Georges, Bermuda
Wednesday, December 22nd, 9:45 A.M.

Cynic: A man who when he smells flowers
looks around for a coffin.

~ H. L. MENCKEN

L ee shuffled up the dock from the boathouse, continuing to mumble and pray to himself. Another fog bank had rolled in, and most of St. Georges had once again disappeared. As Lee entered Kings Square, the West Tower of St. Paul's with its clock was still visible. The white masonry buildings of St. Georges, many built in the seventeenth century, had a ghostly appearance. The town appeared deserted. Most of the shops and pubs hadn't yet opened for the day.

The heavy wooden doors to the church stood open. Lee quickly ascended the stone stairs and stepped inside. The sanctuary was dark.

Before Lee could enter, he was intercepted by a young woman.

"Emanuel?" she asked.

"Um, yes," replied Lee.

"Father Allen is expecting you." She had a very heavy English accent. "This way." She directed Lee to a door on the left side of the sanctuary.

Lee smiled, nodded, and approached the door that she held open.

"Please be seated. Father Allen will join you momentarily."

Lee sat in a heavy wooden chair padded with a purple velvet back and seat in front of a large mahogany desk. He felt as if he'd stepped into a museum. The desk and bookcases were of dark wood, and all the upholstery was dark purple with gold trim. A globe and stack of books sat on a side table. A large wooden cross, also in dark wood, hung from the wall behind the desk. No computer, or any kind of electronic device, including a phone, was visible. The only light in the room came from a lamp on the desk.

Father Allen wasn't long in coming. He entered the room through a small door in the wall behind the desk. Lee started to rise.

"Don't get up." He smiled as he approached. "I'm glad you're safe," he said as he shook Lee's hand. "We prayed for you."

"Well, thank you," said Lee, not knowing what else to say.

"I can tell by the expression on your face that you're confused by all this. Still a skeptic." He turned away from Lee. "I was, also. I still am in some ways."

Lee brightened. "You're right," he said, "I really don't know what to make of all of this."

"I'm sure that David told you some of the story."

Lee closed his eyes. "David certainly told me some stories."

Father Allen smiled again and nodded as he pulled his chair around to face Lee. "I grew up on this island but left in my early twenties and didn't return for many years. I didn't accept the things that my father, a devoutly religious man, told me growing up. Strange things happen here." He shrugged. "They always have. It's Bermuda. My father tried to explain them in a way that put all the pieces together, that connected them, but he really couldn't." He sighed. "He told me that people come here thinking that they're looking for pirates' gold or the Lost City of Atlantis but that they're really looking for what they had lost. I didn't understand what he was trying to tell me. I was a rebellious young man, so I left the island. I tried it my way." He smiled somewhat ruefully. "The world finally broke me. I felt a calling and turned to the church. Not here, in a parish in North Carolina. I became a priest. After my mother passed, my father became more insistent that I return to Bermuda, so I came home."

Lee tried not to listen. "Too much. Too much," Lee muttered, feeling overwhelmed.

Father Allen smiled, "Would you like some coffee?" "No," said Lee.

The priest continued. "I asked my father for proof of what he'd told me. He provided it." He waited. Lee didn't respond.

"Your patient in the reinsurance business, the one who travels back and forth between Bermuda and Portland, the one with the dreams. Frank, came to me, saying that he needed to talk with someone."

"Is that how you know about the dreams?"

"Yes."

"Before I left for Europe, he insisted on meeting me at night. But when I got to his winter rental, the house had burned to the ground and he was nowhere to be found. A few days later, he called my office, saying that he was okay and would talk with me when I returned. So, what was that all about?" Lee sounded irritated.

"They were making an effort, albeit an unsuccessful one, to communicate with you."

Lee closed his eyes. Here we go again with 'They.' "Who the hell— excuse me, Father—are 'They'?"

Father Allen deflected his question. "I . . . I cannot explain that in any way that would be helpful, or even believable, to you. No more than my father could explain that to me. But I think that you'll understand more about all of this before you reach Boston. The world is badly out of balance, and they, along with others, are trying to restore . . ."

"Yes, yes, Father, but what has that got to do with me getting home?" He stared at the priest. "I'd be the first to agree that the world is, as you say, out of balance. The one percent controls the lives of the ninety-nine percent. Our world culture is in its adolescence. And like an adolescent, we're self-centered," his voice rose; his impatience was showing. "We want what we want when we want it. And right now, I want to go home. So, what does all that have to do with me getting home?"

"A great deal. It's very important that you reach Boston and deliver the package. I'm sorry, Dr. Brazil, that I'm unable to explain this better." He looked away for a moment then back at Lee. "I can only say that the package you carry could help restore balance to our world . . . indeed, our universe. It must not fall into the wrong hands."

"And whose hands might those be?" asked Lee, feeling and sounding confused and exasperated.

Father Allen pretended not to hear him.

Lee was beginning to have some serious doubts about Father Allen's sanity and his own. Certainly, the human race's culture of violence and greed had put the world out of balance, to use Father Allen's words, but what could possibly be in the package that would change that?

"People may soon have the ability to spread the worst of our culture to other parts of the universe," Father Allen said. "This cannot happen. We cannot permit it," he said forcefully. "What you carry could help prevent that from happening."

Lee gave up. He didn't understand any of it, but he decided that if Father Allen could help him get to Boston, that's what was important— nothing else.

"Well, Father, I agree with you, I want to get home." An uncomfortable silence ensued. Father Allen stood up. "An old friend of yours is here and has agreed to help us." "And who is that?" asked Lee impatiently.

"Before I ask her to join us, I must tell you that she knows little of what we've discussed, and the less she knows, the safer she'll be. This brought her here." From his shirt pocket, the priest drew a small gold cross with seven green stones and laid it on the side table next to Lee.

"This is the cross that David spoke of?" asked Lee with interest.

"Yes. It was her grandfather's."

"She's from Maine?"

"Yes. She came today to return the cross to our church. She didn't realize that it was directing here for another purpose."

"I've explained that you need her help to return to Boston, that you've gotten into some trouble in your work for the United States government. She's aware of your involvement with these government 'projects.' She said you'd talked with her years ago about them."

"Oh, God." Lee finally remembered the cross. She'd worn it frequently when they were together many, many years ago. She'd talked of her grandfather and Bermuda. He remembered.

"It took some convincing, but she has agreed to help us."

Lee stood up quickly and nearly lost his balance.

"Are you alright, Dr. Brazil?" asked Father Allen, rising himself. "If so, I'll ask her to come in."

Lee's heart pounded; his throat felt parched. "Yes, yes. Please" was all he could get out.

Father Allen nodded. He stepped to the door through which he'd entered and opened it.

"Joann, will you please join us?"

CHAPTER 26

St. Paul's
St. Georges, Bermuda
Wednesday, December 22nd, 10:23 A.M.

Anxiety weighs down the heart, but a good word cheers it.

~ Proverbs

Joann stepped into the room slowly. She seemed almost embarrassed to be there, avoiding eye contact with both Lee and Father Allen.

"Joann," Lee spoke first, but he could say nothing else.

Father Allen broke the silence. "Please." He directed her to the chair next to Lee's. Lee hadn't moved. As she approached, he reached out to take her hand. She let him.

She was still a beautiful woman, a woman, Lee had always thought, who bloomed wherever she planted herself. In her early seventies, she looked much younger, though her hair was finally graying. Small and still trim, she dressed like a New Englander: dark blue blazer, white shirt, jeans, and running shoes.

Lee hadn't seen her in years. They'd met over forty years before; he a young psychologist focused on building his practice, she a school social worker with plans to open her own business, they fell in love and lived together for a few years. But the energy faded. Time and other relationships came and went before they reconnected years later.

When they realized that anything more than friendship offered only confusion and possible pain, they took things no further. They talked occasionally: a phone call, a card, an e-mail, maybe even an occasional dinner, but when she left New England to be close to family in Florida, they lost contact. For years. But a couple of weeks before leaving for Europe, Lee, for some reason, felt that he should send her a Christmas card. To his surprise, she replied with a New Year's card.

"Joann," he said again. This time, she looked up and made eye contact. "How have you been?"

"Better than you, apparently," she said with a smile. She was a quiet person with a quick wit.

Lee nodded and returned the smile. A sense of relief, peace, filled his body. In the middle of all of this . . . this craziness, he suddenly felt at ease. Safe. It was her smile. The sound of her voice. It had always been that way. They didn't need to have long, labored talks about their feelings. They just needed to look at each other. It was simple. He remembered.

"I like the new look," she said. "Who's your stylist?" "Edward," Lee said and laughed.

"I'm afraid that I must interrupt," Father Allen said. "Your ship sails this afternoon. Martha has arranged for a taxi to take you back to the dock. Here are your papers, Emanuel. Your passport. Joann will help you through customs. You must keep these on." He handed Lee a pair of sunglasses and a cap. "You have a history of migraines, and you're having one. When you're in your cabin, which adjoins Joann's, she'll call the ship's doctor, who will see you in your cabin and arrange a medical excuse. You're sailing back light, without passengers, so your absence won't be a problem."

He looked at Lee and said emphatically, "Stay in your cabin until you arrive in Boston. Customs there won't be a problem, and they tell me that the dock is only a few blocks from an Agent Jennings' office. You know the address. Go there directly. Jennings will be expecting you."

Lee looked down at the sunglasses, cap, and passport then nodded.

Father Allen herded them toward the door. "Say little in the taxi. Michael, the driver, is a talker and a gossip. He'll entertain you with his stories about Bermuda. Joann can explain that you're not feeling well."

He took Joanne's hands. "Thank you so very much for your help and for the beautiful cross."

She nodded. "I'm sure it's what my grandfather would have wanted."

"You may not know how right you are," the priest replied.

He turned to Lee. "Take care, friend. May God be with you and us."

"Well, yes," said Lee. "And thank you for helping me to . . . get home."

"Yes, Martha, we're coming." Father Allen replied to a knock on the door and looked down at the sunglasses and the cap, which Lee quickly donned. He then escorted Lee and Joann to the main door of the church. "Michael is waiting. Godspeed."

CHAPTER 27

Bermuda
Wednesday, December 22nd, 10:46 A.M.

Their destination, Kings Wharf and the Royal Naval dockyard, was over twenty-five miles away on the opposite end of the island. As Father Allen had said, Michael was a talker. But he was also full of questions. Where were they from? What brought them to Bermuda?

Joann answered as best she could and explained that Emanuel was not feeling well, which, from Lee's perspective, was the truth.

As they left St. Georges, Michael pointed out the sights: the unfinished church, the State House. They by-passed the modern city of Hamilton, Bermuda's capital, and followed the coastline, passing beautiful beaches and driving through other small villages that looked similar to St. Georges. Lee paid little attention to the travelogue. He closed his eyes and tried to understand the events of the last twenty-four hours. But it was all too much; he could make no sense of it. With the early afternoon sun on his face, the drone of conversation, and the motion of the taxi, Lee drifted off. When they arrived at the dock, Joann had to shake him awake.

"Emanuel!"

"Huh?" He felt somewhat dazed for a moment.

"We're here." Joann got out of the cab, paid Michael, and thanked him.

Lee stumbled out of the taxi and followed Joann up the dock. It was a beautiful afternoon. The sky was clear, the ocean a bright metallic blue.

The Saint was the only cruise ship in the boatyard. Built in the late 1990s, she was "old" and, although she could house over two thousand passengers and a thousand crew, by "modern standards" she was small.

Only one customs officer stood at the ship entrance. Joann smiled, showed both of their passports, and explained that Emanuel was dealing with a migraine. Lee nodded, and they gained entry to the ship.

The entryway was deserted. They boarded the elevator to Deck 4. When they exited, Joann directed them down the hall. The ship was eerily quiet.

"Where is everyone?" asked Joann. "It's like a ghost ship." "You may be right," said Lee.

"I'll see you in a minute," she said, sliding her keycard into the door.

"Okay," said Lee, waiting for something else; he didn't know what. He fumbled through his shirt and pants pockets, finally finding his own card in his jacket pocket. He slipped it in and pushed the door open slowly. A stateroom with an ocean view, meaning he had a porthole. He scanned the room: Small bath, microwave, double bed, chair.

Lee opened the door in answer to a knock, but no one was there. The knock came again, and he realized that Joann was knocking on the door that adjoined the two cabins. Lee opened it.

"What were you doing?" she demanded.

Lee was somewhat taken aback. Suddenly, he recalled that fear always came out as anger with her. She was afraid. Why? "Just looking over the place."

"Well, you're going to find that this is the weirdest ship you've ever been on, with the weirdest people. I've been on cruise ships before, but never one like this. I almost had the driver take me to the airport this morning for a flight back to Boston. Maybe I should have." She took a deep breath. "Now, tell me; what's going on? What kind of a mess are you in?"

"I don't know," said Lee. "I'm as confused as you. Maybe more."

"Well, if you don't know, I surely don't. I just answered an ad on the Internet. You know how I hate the holidays. I thought it would be an opportunity to get away for a few days and make some extra money, not that I need any, taking care of a couple of kids. It all sounded good, so I e- mailed the couple my résumé and, within a few hours, I got a positive response and directions to the dock. The next day, I got a FedEx with a train ticket to Boston and a round-trip ticket on *The Saint*." She walked over to the window. "Thought that I could see Bermuda, which I've always avoided for some reason. And that cross."

"Oh, yes," Lee managed to squeeze in.

"For some reason, I felt like I had to return it to my grandfather's church. Strange." She turned to face Lee. "You know, I took the cross to a jeweler once. I asked him if he could tell me what the stones were. I thought they might be emeralds. He couldn't. He said they weren't emeralds, but he had no idea what they were or where they were from." Lee looked away and changed the subject. "So, what's wrong with the ship and people?"

Joann looked out the porthole, silent for a moment. "I . . . don't really know. I mean, the passengers aren't . . . normal. They seem surprised and fascinated by everything." She shook her head. "The television, my cell phone, you name it. I don't know what rocks they've been under for the last fifty years. Some said that they were excited, because they were going Home. Bermuda is their home, I guess?"

"And the kids?" asked Lee.

"Two little boys. They're fine, but they keep talking about a storm and being on a yacht, taking a trip around the world. The yacht had a strange name . . . uh, *The Empress* . . . no, *The Enchanter*."

"*The Enchantress*?" asked Lee.

"Yes. I believe that was it.""Built in the mid-twenties. Lost in the Caribbean in the mid-sixties." "How do you know that?" she snapped.

"I've always been a fan of Maine maritime history; you know

that." "Oh, yes," she replied, remembering.

"There was a family aboard. A husband and wife and two children, and a small crew." Lee began to pace. "Authorities never found wreckage of the ship. They all just disappeared."

"You do know how crazy that sounds, right? And even if it wasn't, what does that have to do with us?" She stared at Lee again.

"I don't know," said Lee. "Nothing I guess."

"Well, there's nothing I can do about it. It's beyond me." She turned away from him. "So, I'm just going to be a good girl and do what Father Allen requested." She moved toward the adjoining door. "As promised, I'll report you to sick bay." She pushed Lee through the doorway. "Now, back to your cabin and look sick."

"I really don't think that will be difficult."

CHAPTER 28

The Saint
Kings Wharf, Bermuda
Wednesday, December 22nd, 12:14 P.M.

Lee closed the door to Joann's room and surveyed his cabin. A double bed, neatly made by Emanuel, he assumed. Clothing stacked on the dresser. Pants with pants, shirts with shirts. A place for everything, and everything in its place. He suddenly felt very much alone. He didn't like the feeling. It scared him.

He made his way to the bathroom and switched on the light, reacting with a start when he saw his image in the mirror. He was still having difficulty seeing himself as a younger man . . . with hair. It was like an out- of-body experience, like watching himself from deep inside the body he saw in the mirror. He unwrapped a plastic glass, filled it to the brim, and gulped the water. He looked again with anticipation and scanned the image slowly.

His self-examination was interrupted by a knock at the cabin door. He swung his body around, missed the step-down from the bathroom, and almost fell. Regaining his balance, he stumbled toward the door.

The knock came again, louder. "This is Dr. Sherman," a voice said. "Please open the door." Lee positioned himself behind the door and complied. Dr. Sherman entered the room cautiously. When he didn't see anyone, he peered around the corner of the door and smiled.

Dr. Sherman was tall, with a full head of black hair streaked with gray. Trim and fit looking, he appeared to take his own advice regarding self- care. Without a word, he directed Lee toward the bed.

Lee stopped at its edge.

"Please," said the doctor, "I can help."

Lee didn't respond.

The doctor whispered, "And, no, you're not the Emanuel who left the ship this morning."

Lee turned toward him, alarmed.

"But I'll help you as a favor to my old friend, Father Allen. Please, sit." He patted the bed then drew a chair from the table and sat down. Lee seated himself on the bed's edge.

"You're my first patient since we left Boston three days ago. Strange cruise. No one has been to my office, not even for a Band-Aid." He reached into his medical bag, pulled out a prescription pad, and began to write.

"Here." He handed Lee a medical excuse slip. "You won't have to work until we arrive in Boston." He stood. "Have Joann give this to the chief steward."

Lee couldn't speak English with a Latino accent, and his Spanish was horrible, so he'd planned to say as little as possible. His silence didn't seem to matter to the doctor. He knew Lee wasn't who he was pretending to be.

"You must stay in your cabin. Joann can bring you your meals."

Lee decided to risk it and blurted in English, "What's all this about?"

Dr. Sherman smiled for a second time. "I don't really know. We have a new captain—Wormell is his name—and a number of new crew. They appear to care little about what I'm doing and, I would assume, what you're up to. They don't seem very friendly. I think they're avoiding me." "Wormell," said Lee. Same as the captain of the ill-fated *Carol Deering*.

"Yes," said Dr. Sherman, showing interest. "You know him?"

"No, no." Lee felt like he was blushing He wasn't ready to explore that one, so he changed the subject. "What are you doing on this ship?"

"I couldn't stand retirement. My wife died a few years ago. A rare form of brain cancer." He stroked his chin. "It's becoming more common because of all the electronic devices we seem obsessed with. Anyway, they needed a doc, and I needed to get away. So, I do this. It's quite boring at times. I've hardly talked to a soul since we left Boston."

"Microwaves and cancer. That's still is a pretty controversial issue, isn't it?" asked Lee.

He shrugged. "For some it is, and I would guess that many people and corporations would like to keep it that way. I just know what my colleagues in oncology tell me."

A buzzing interrupted him. "Well, finally, someone wants to see me." He took out his cell phone and looked at it with interest. "Speak of the devil. It's the captain."

He turned to Lee. "So . . . Emanuel, I wish you good fortune. I have no idea why you're so important to Father Allen, but I don't need to know." Dr. Sherman moved toward the door then turned and smiled.

"Work on your Spanish."

CHAPTER 29

The Saint
King's Wharf, Bermuda
Wednesday, December 22nd, 1:06 P.M.

There must be virtue in brilliance followed by
stupidity, for man is alternatively brilliant and
stupid, and man is a creation of God.

~ KURT VONNEGUT,
Player Piano

Lee started to knock on the door to Joann's room but stopped himself. He needed to stop. He needed to be alone. Time alone had been in short supply since he'd left the hotel in Paris. It had only been two days.

No, not even that. A little over a day. God, it felt like a week, a month.

He lay down on the bed and thought of Liz and Dru. It was two days before the first night of Hanukkah—the Festival of Lights. They would light the candles, give their gifts, but he might not be with them. He couldn't call them. He couldn't call anyone. Liz would assume the worst. She always did. But there was nothing to do about it.

He checked the inside pocket of his coveralls. The package was still there. In another day and a half, he would, hopefully, be in Boston and could hand it over to Jennings and be done with this whole thing. He wouldn't do this again; he was too old for all of this foolishness. He would tell Jennings not to ask again. If he wanted to lock him up again, so be it.

And all that business about the *Carol Deering*, the dreams. Was he supposed to believe all that? And Father Allen—how was it that such a nice guy was involved in all this craziness? And the computer, Edward. Too much. Too much. He closed his eyes.

Lee awakened with a start. Someone was at his door. He froze. The door opened. It was Joann with a tray of food.

"You missed our departure," she said. "It's really a beautiful harbor. The old fort, the lighthouse. But you slept through it."

Lee didn't respond.

"Are you okay?"

He nodded.

"It's getting late, and the employee dining room closes at seven. I hope this is okay."

"I'm sure it will be." Lee said distractedly. "I'm not really that hungry."

She put the tray on a table by the bed and sat next to him. "You look tired. You sure you're okay? Did things go alright with Dr. Sherman?"

Lee continued to look away. "Yes, yes. I'm sorry. I'm not very good company. I'm just trying to understand . . . well, you know . . ."

"Hey, you and me both." She paused then asked, "Do you know anything about the Singularity?"

"Not much. I did hear Clayton talk about it on NPR. Why?"

"I overheard a conversation in the dining room coming down from Boston. Two men at the captain's table were talking about when a single computer will be smarter than the entire human race."

"Yeah. I think that's what the term 'Singularity' refers to."

"One of the men said that that day is fast approaching and, when it arrives, will be the undoing of the human race . . . maybe the entire universe. He said that the moral development of the human race wasn't keeping up with the development of technology."

Lee smiled nervously. "Well, we *have* done a poor job of programming ourselves in that area." He stood and walked to the porthole. "We can't teach machines to teach other machines to behave better than we do."

He turned to Joann again. "Remember that Vonnegut novel, one of those he wrote in the late '50s? What was it . . . Yes, *Player Piano*." He concentrated on remembering. "Engineers had designed machines that could do most human work. They took good care of the people, who were well fed and housed but did nothing meaningful. Those who wanted to stay busy were consigned to 'busywork' and entertained themselves through organizing and participating in social clubs. Like we occupy ourselves with Facebook and the rest."

"Oh, yes," said Joann. "It does sound similar to today's world. I guess we could just replace social clubs with social media."

"And people finally revolted against the machines," Lee continued. "Unfortunately, it failed, just like *Player Piano* when it was first published."

"I remember," said Joann. "The story certainly doesn't have a happy ending." She frowned. "The man also said that these new machines could develop the technology to explore the entire universe."

Lee walked back to the bed and sat down. "I assume that might be possible. If so, we could spread some of our best cultural aspects to the entire universe. Especially those we focus so much of our attention on, like violence and greed."

"Yes. I think that's what he was talking about."

"We do have a legacy of both. I mean, the American frontier was a combat zone, with violence usually driven by greed, wasn't it?" Lee's voice rose.

Joann nodded.

"But I'm sure the corporations could care less about all that," said Lee with a smirk. "The main goal of most is to produce a profit, and the first corporation to develop such a machine would certainly reap those." Lee sighed deeply. "Think about it: to develop the first computer smarter than the entire human race, than all human beings combined. In addition to solving the problems of time and space, such a machine could solve the problem of mortality. We might become immortal."

"I doubt a machine could do that," said Joann.

"Yes, you're probably right about that," said Lee with a faint smile. Neither spoke for a few minutes, and the silence became awkward.

"Well, I don't know what that has to do with us," said Joann. "I'll just be glad to get back to Boston and home. I think 'll turn in now."

"Oh, okay," said Lee absently, still in thought. "I guess I will too."

Joann stood. "It's a beautiful night. Clear, calm seas."

Lee didn't respond immediately. Finally, he said, "I would love to go topside with you, but Father Allen said I should stay . . . I . . ."

"Okay," she snapped. "I'll bring you breakfast in the morning. Two eggs over easy, and sausage patties, not links. And, of course, OJ, right?"

Lee nodded and sighed. "I'm very sorry we had to meet under . . ." "Me, too, but such is life." She smiled and quickly closed the door.

He picked at the meal she'd brought and thought about the past. He and Joann had taken a cruise many years ago. A very short one. That was all they could afford in those days. Lee remembered the calm, the moon on the water. So many years ago. He put the meal aside and lay back on the bed.

Ultra-intelligent machines had been just the stuff of fiction in those days, but now . . . the Singularity pushed its way back into his thoughts. "Oh, God, what a disaster it could be."

CHAPTER 30

The Saint
Kings Wharf, Bermuda
Wednesday, December 22nd, 3:17 P.M.

Hope: The poor man's bread.

~ George Herbert

It didn't take Jeff long to discover the female American accomplice. Only five women were aboard: the cruise director, the director of childcare, one chef, and two cooks. The crew was mostly Latino and Indian. The best candidate was the childcare director. She was new. No one knew her.

Jeff had watched her leave the ship that morning. The three women in food services didn't' have shore leave, due to the ship's quick turn-around. The cruise director had left with one of the officers, and they seemed to have things besides espionage on their minds. When Jeff observed Joann returning that afternoon with another crewman, he was convinced that she was the one. Both she and the other crewman, Emanuel Rodriguez, seemed very uncomfortable with everyone: the taxi driver, security, customs.

Jeff talked to the head steward later that evening and found that Dr. Sherman had written a medical excuse for Emanuel for the entire return trip. Apparently, he had a bad headache.

That might land someone in sick bay for a day, but not the entire cruise, Jeff thought. Very unusual. He must be the guy. When Emanuel left his cabin, he'd search it. If the package wasn't there or in the cabin safe, he must be carrying it on his person. Jeff assumed that he wouldn't take the chance of leaving it with Joann or hiding it in her cabin. He just had to wait for his opportunity to get into Emanuel's cabin.

CHAPTER 31

St. Paul's Church Cemetery
St. Georges, Bermuda
Wednesday, December 22nd, 4:15 P.M.

The home of God is with mortals. He will dwell with them.

~ Revelations

D avid came her often at this time of day, to visit his family. Robert, his younger son, seventy-seven at his death; James, seventy-nine; and his wife, eighty-five. An empty space next to his wife waited for him. He wondered when he would fill it. Life extension had felt like a gift at first, but the last thirty years had made it a curse.

He paused to watch the sun set before going into the church. It reminded him of another sunset he'd seen almost a hundred years ago from the wheelhouse of the *Carol Deering*.

He'd come to see Father Allen in person rather than use an electronic device, because the message might be intercepted: Lee, aka Emanuel, and Joann had gotten through customs and were safely aboard *The Saint*. He and the priest had put their pieces of the puzzle in place. What the bigger picture would show once others inserted their pieces, David didn't know.

The Saint
Atlantic Ocean
Thursday, December 23rd, 1:58 A.M.

At first, Lee thought that it was morning or he was dreaming.

A faint blue light flooded the entire cabin. He sat up. It was still there, spilling into the room through the porthole. Lee struggled to his feet and stumbled toward the source. Might the bright blue light be a searchlight on another ship? No. It was high in the sky; stars winked faintly below it.

He couldn't judge how far it was. Joann had talked about a strange light in the sky on the night before they'd docked in Bermuda. Lee started to knock on her door but didn't. He glanced at his watch. 2:00 A.M. He could get a better look at whatever it was from the deck. He thought to dress but realized that he was still dressed from the day before.

He knew he shouldn't leave, but the compulsion to go topside was too strong. He carefully opened the door. The hall was empty. Eerily quiet. He walked slowly and silently toward the stairs and mounted the first step. His right hand took the rail, one step after another, then a second set of stairs. He turned the latch for the starboard exit and cracked open the door but didn't exit yet.

The deck was bathed in light, as he imagined it might look with a clear sky and a full moon. The only other lights were from the deck bar. But the bar had been closed for at least an hour. The tables were empty. No, wait; in the corner, at the far end of the bar, in the shadows, Lee thought he saw the silhouette of a man—an older man with bushy hair and a long beard. He rubbed his eyes and tried to focus. Yes, someone was there.

Lee pushed open the door to the deck and inched along the wall, staying in the shadow of the overhanging deck. The figure at the table was facing the light. Lee continued his silent approach. What the hell are you doing? He asked himself. I don't know, he replied. He was a few feet from the figure.

"Lee, come sit with me." The voice was familiar. It sounded like Griff, an old friend since the Seventies. They'd worked together when Griff had decided that grant writing was his second calling after he'd burned out temporarily with the church and God.

"Come," the figure said again. "We have much to talk about and little time." The source of the voice turned to face Lee. It was . . . Griff. But how could that be?

"Sit down, my old friend."

Lee cautiously took a seat, without taking his eyes off of Griff.

"You're quite pale."

Lee said nothing.

"You don't look well."

"Should I? I'm talking to a dead man."

Griff chuckled. The sound was familiar. He had always appreciated Lee's attempts at humor in tense situations.

It *is* Griff, Lee admitted reluctantly. He looked much as he had the last time Lee had seen him, a few days before he and the *John Wesley II* sailed out of Casco Bay. He hadn't aged. That was three, almost four, years ago.

Griff still had his beard, now white. And a full head of hair, but thinning. Average build and weight for a man now in his late eighties.

"We're not alone in this universe; we're all connected," Griff said as he turned to Lee.

"Yes, I've been getting that distinct impression in the last few days."

Griff smiled. "There are billions of galaxies out there." He waved toward the light off starboard. "Billions. It would be foolish to believe otherwise, wouldn't it? Why has it taken us so long to accept that life exists on other worlds, too?"

Lee didn't have an answer.

Griff shrugged. "I suppose the same reason it took us so long to accept that our world wasn't at the center of the universe. That the universe didn't revolve around us."

Lee put his hand on Griff's shoulder. It felt solid. "Griff, what . . . what . . .. are you real?" Lee asked. He could see *that* this was Griff, but he was still trying to comprehend *how* his friend could possibly be there. "Are you part of a dream?"

"What do you think? Don't I sound real? Don't I feel real?"

"I don't know, maybe. I could be imagining all this." Lee withdrew his hand. "Are you alive?"

"In what dimension?" asked Griff, chuckling.

Lee felt even more bewildered and started to rise.

"Forgive my question, old friend. I'm here talking. Isn't that enough?"

"Yes, but..."

"Lee," Griff interrupted, "I can't explain all of this in the time that we have. I can't answer all your questions." "I don't understand. You're dead. We held a memorial service . . ."

Griff stopped him. "They sent me to explain to you what you must do. They thought I could make it easier for you to understand."

"Must do what? And who the hell are 'they'? Explain that to me!" He tried to rise again but couldn't.

"Calm down, Lee, and listen to me," Griff said firmly. "I don't pretend to understand them fully, but I believe that they're an old intelligence who have been in our universe since it began. Many of them walk among us."

Lee looked away.

"They plucked me from the sea when I was drowning. They also saved the crews of the *Carol Deering*, *The Enchantress*, and hundreds of others. If they hadn't intervened, we all would have perished. They mean us no harm, but they're not sure that we feel the same."

Lee's eyes came to rest on the bright, metallic blue light off starboard. "What harm can we inflict on them?" Lee grumbled. "We've spent most of the last ten thousand years trying to kill each other."

"True, but the problem isn't what we've *done*; it's what we might soon be able to do: The Singularity, the computer that we may soon build."

Lee objected. "We're still in our technological adolescence, and we'll be lucky to survive it without killing ourselves. Most civilizations in the universe would likely have blown themselves up soon after figuring out $E=MC^2$."

"But we *are* poised to take a giant step forward."

"Yes, I know," Lee agreed. "A lot of people are talking about it. Congress just appropriated money to fund the project."

"But, as we both know, our race isn't ready for this," Griff warned. Lee nodded.

Griff continued, "We're mere babes when it comes to moral development. Yet, we're a very special species, made from some of the rarest elements in the universe. We dream beautiful dreams, but . . ."

". . . we can create horrible nightmares."

Griff touched Lee's shoulder. "They can't risk us spreading those nightmares throughout the universe that we all share. Lee, please understand: they're tired of being ignored, discounted, seen only as the stuff of science fiction and no more. They'll do something very soon to get the attention of the world."

He took Lee's hand. "Other forces in our universe will be neither as patient nor as benign."

"I can understand that," Lee responded, "but what are you expecting me to do about it?"

"You're carrying a very important package to Boston for Agent Jennings."

"I am?" said Lee, remembering Father Allen's words.

"Do you know what it contains?" asked Griff.

"No, but I suppose it has something to do with the spy game," Lee said with contempt. "A list of secret codes or something like that."

Griff looked at him sternly. "Lee, the Cold War is over. The spying that goes on now—and there's a lot of it—is one corporation spying on another. One mega-company trying to steal the other mega-corporation's secrets. And what do they want more than anything else?" he asked.

"I suppose the plans for the next advancement in IT," ventured Lee. "The next super-computer."

"Exactly."

"Please don't use that word. You sound like Jennings."

"Lee, pay attention." Griff said impatiently. "The disk you carry does have secret codes on it—for the next giant step in IT. The ultimate super- computer. Hollocore wants to make sure that you and the package reach Boston. But as you're aware, some of its competitors would like to see you dead and have the disk."

Lee nodded. "Yeah, I'm well aware of that."

"In a few days, our government will ask for proposals to finish building the supercomputer that the Eu began. Hollocore has already 'arranged' to receive the contract. They'll do what companies have done for centuries: Have the government pay them to do what they want to do anyway and then reap the profits of having done it. They *definitely* want you and the disk to reach Boston safely. So why kill you?" Griff smiled.

Lee pulled the package out of his vest pocket. "So that's what the *Greatest Hits of Rock 'n Roll* really is," Lee said with a hint of awe.

Griff nodded. "But we have a plan." He produced a package and laid it on the table next to Lee's. They were identical. "Our disk has similar codes but also has a number of viruses that Hollocore won't be able to detect. Remember Stuxnet and Flame, the cyberweapons that the U.S. and Israel used to screw up and slow down the development of Iran's nuclear program? Our program will keep Hollocore busy for years trying to understand what's wrong. It will set back their plans for decades and give us more time to . . . grow up, develop our moral compass."

"Good luck with that," said Lee, skeptically. "So I must . . ."

A blast of wind across the deck sent some debris flying and interrupted his thought.

Griff rose. "So, my old friend, *you* must reach Boston, and *I* must go."

The air around the ship became more turbulent. A stack of bar napkins on the next table flew into the air and rained down like large pieces of confetti. The bottles and glassware rattled as a humming sound grew louder.

A large black mass lowered onto the ship's helipad. Barely visible from the bar, the pad was about a hundred yards toward the stern.

Lee found his sea legs and stood up. He turned, but Griff was gone, as was one of the packages. The bright light off starboard had also disappeared. The dark had returned. The only illumination was a light hanging over the bar and the ship's navigation lights.

Lee grabbed the remaining package and shoved it into his breast pocket.

He backed into the shadows and retraced his steps to the stairwell.

The wind subsided, and the humming became a low groan. The cabin door of the helicopter slid open, and a figure slipped onto the deck. Three others followed, carrying what appeared to be automatic weapons.

The speed of Lee's retreat increased. He slipped through the door to the stairwell and moved quickly down the stairs to the next deck then to the next. His heart pounded in his ears; his breathing was rapid. Taking two steps at a time, he didn't look back.

When he reached the fourth deck and turned toward the exit, a strange sensation ran through his entire body. It began as a sharp pain in his lower back and moved up, spreading into his arms and his neck, and, finally, his head. He blacked out.

The Saint
Boston Harbor, Boston, Massachusetts
Friday, December 24th, 2:09 A.M.

Love bears all things, believes all things,
hopes all things, endures all things.

~I Corinthians

"Lee, Lee," a soft, gentle voice said.

When he didn't respond, the voice persisted and was more emphatic. "Lee."

Someone was shaking his arm and saying his name for a fourth time. Lee opened his eyes slowly.

"I'm awake, honey. I was just resting my eyes."

Joann laughed. "I think you were doing more than that. If you're that tired," she sounded sympathetic, "why don't you just go to bed? It's okay."

"No, no," Lee protested. "I love sitting here with you. Besides, it's cooler out here than inside. It reminds me of a July night in the South." He wiped away the beads of sweat on his forehead with the back of his hand.

They were sitting on the porch of a small cottage they'd bought a year before. It had taken every spare penny they could put together to make the down payment. It was what she'd wanted. What they both had wanted. It was on a small lake, just north of Portland. Near their work. It was perfect. They could, to quote the realtor, "go up and even out. Make it into a real home." But it was fine and as much as they needed, at least for now. There were no children. Not yet.

"I love it here," Lee said again.

"I told you that you would," said Joann. "I'm glad we brought this thing back from Tennessee." She was referring to an old glider that they'd taken from Lee's grandparents' home.

"I'm sure that the people who bought the place would have sold it or given it away."

"I'm sorry that I tried to talk you out of renting the trailer and hauling it back. I really do like it."

The glider squeaked with each rotation.

"I'll oil it this weekend," said Lee.

"It's okay. I think it gives it character," Joann chuckled.

Whether it squeaked or not didn't really matter. They were sitting on their porch, rocking back and forth in their glider, looking at their lake. Well, actually, the community's lake, but that didn't matter, either. They closed their eyes and continued to rock. Time passed. It was getting late.

"Lee," the voice came again.

"I was just . . ."

"I know, but it's getting late, and we both have to work tomorrow." Joann had kept her job as a school social worker, not so much because she liked the job—though she did—but for the insurance. Lee was just starting his practice. They wanted a good insurance policy, because they would soon need it. Joann was pregnant. Lightning flashed to the east over the ocean. Thunder rumbled in the distance.

Joann stood up. "I wish it would just go ahead and rain."

Lee got up and put his arm around her. "It will soon, and that will cool things down. We'll need a blanket." He shook his head. "Maine weather."

They undressed and slipped between the clean, fresh sheets. She snuggled close. The sheets were cool against their skin and, for a few seconds, soothed the evening heat. Lee loved how they felt, how she felt. He buried his face in her hair. She smelled so good. They drifted off to sleep.

When Lee woke up, Joann was sitting in a chair next to the bed. The room was filled with a faint blue light. The moon, he thought. The rain must have come, and the sky had cleared. But something was wrong. Joann was dressed and . . . so was he.

"What's wrong, honey?" he asked, alarmed.

Joann shook herself awake. She opened her eyes and looked at Lee.

"Well, sleeping beauty, you've returned." Lee sat up.

"What are you talking about? What time is it? We don't have to get up yet, do we?"

"I think it's about five o'clock," said Joann, "and you're right; we don't dock until six. But I would imagine we're in the harbor."

She got up and walked to the porthole. "I saw a strange light earlier tonight, but it's gone now."

"What? My first patient isn't until nine, and you don't have to be at school until 7:30."

"He said you'd be confused."

Lee raised his voice. "Who said that?"

"Dr. Sherman. He said that it would take twenty-four hours, and it's been just about that."

"Who's Sherman?"

Just as the words left his mouth, Lee remembered where he was. He swung his feet over the edge of the bed and onto the floor.

"Hold on. Let me help you. You haven't been on your feet in a day."

"It's okay. I'm just going to sit here for a few minutes," said Lee, running his hand through his hair.

Joann sat down and switched on a lamp near the bed. The light stung Lee's eyes, so he closed them again.

"How did I get here?"

"Will you listen to me and believe what I'm going to tell you? Because I find it all a bit hard to believe myself."

"Okay, okay. I trust you. Tell me." He was becoming impatient.

"About three o'clock yesterday morning . . ."

"Yesterday?"

"Yes, Lee. You slept through the last twenty-four hours. You've lost a day. Now, please, just let me finish."

"Yes, yes, go on."

"Around three o'clock, I was awakened by a knock at the cabin door. I know that it was about three o'clock . . ."

"Yes, yes, yes. You looked at the clock."

"Sherman was right about you being irritable when you woke up."

"I'm sorry," said Lee. "Please, please do go on."

"I could hear voices in the hall, so I looked out. I could see four men in the hall. They were wearing black jumpsuits with," she paused, thinking, "yes, with 'Hollocore Security' printed on the back. They were dragging some poor fellow down the hall. He was resisting but stopped when they tasered him." She stood up. "One man said something about him being a spy for TransSea. I think that's what he said. TransSea."

Lee nodded. "That makes sense. That's one of their competitors. Another of the lovely corporations running the world."

"What are they doing on this ship?" she asked, turning to face him.

"I have no idea. In fact, I don't have much idea of what's going on, period."

"Well, like I said, the fellow stopped squirming, and they carried him up the steps. I closed the door but, after a few minutes, I heard groaning and a brushing sound against the door. I looked through the peep hole again but couldn't see anyone, so I cracked the door open and found you lying with your back against the door."

Lee remembered. He'd fallen down the steps and was lying on his chest, face down at the bottom. Someone was tugging at his left arm, but his legs were tangled in the railing, and the person was having difficulty turning him over. Before falling, he'd locked his hook around his right arm.

Then he heard a voice: "Go back. Go back, Lee. It's not time. It's not time." For a moment, he thought that his mother was standing in front of him. She'd sailed on this ship a few months before her death. But his vision blurred and he passed out again.

The next thing he heard were voices behind him, the sounds of a scuffle.

The person stopped tugging at his arm.

Joann continued, "So I pulled you into the cabin and called Dr. Sherman. You were talking out of your head. Dr. Sherman helped me get you into bed."

Almost instinctively, Lee felt his breast pocket. It was empty. He tried to stand but couldn't. "Oh, God, where is it?"

"Relax, James Bond. I found it next to you and put it in the cabin safe." Lee still looked terrified. "Well, I've got to have it."

"And you shall, but rest for now. You'll need to be ready to go through customs in a couple of hours." She felt his forehead. "Your fever's gone. Here, drink this." She handed him a glass of water.

He looked at it carefully.

"It's water. For God sakes, Lee, I'm not trying to finish you off. Being poisoned once was enough."

"Poisoned?"

"According to Dr. Sherman."

"How?"

"He wasn't completely sure, but he found a small puncture wound on your lower back."

Lee recalled the sharp pain in his back, and the numbness that spread up his back into his head, before he blacked out.

"He said that the wound could've been made by a dart gun, the type used to bring down large animals, and that the drug was . . . here, he wrote it down." She handed Lee a scrap of paper.

"Oh, yeah, Ketamine or Telazol. That would certainly do it."

"He said you were lucky that it didn't stop your heart." She paused. "And that you'd have very vivid dreams and, when you woke up, would be confused and a bit agitated and have one hell of a hangover."

"Well, he's right on all points."

"Well, you certainly seemed to enjoy whatever you were dreaming. You kept telling me to come back to bed, but I can assure you that nothing happened."

"Oh, I'm sure . . . nothing did." Lee smiled slightly, remembering his dream.

"You were dreaming about us?" she asked, starting to blush.

Lee hesitated. "Well, yes, about the past . . . old times. Very old times." He looked away but he felt the need to turn to her. "The dream was about the life we didn't choose." She was silent.

"It was just a dream," said Lee dismissively. "Oh, I see."

He didn't think that she did, but the conversation was becoming uncomfortable. "I need to finish packing my carry-on. I put your clothes— or Emanuel's—in a bag in your room. I suppose he'll be . . ."

Joann continued on, but Lee wasn't listening. He did as she'd directed earlier: he lay down again and closed his eyes. They were on their porch again. A cool wind came up. They snuggled closer. They watched the moon set over their lake. Lee thought of what might have been and smiled again.

He'd spent too much of his time over the last few years thinking and fantasizing about what might have been. This was an old pattern that he needed to change, but he was going to enjoy it one last time.

CHAPTER 32

The Saint
Boston Harbor, Massachusetts
Friday, December 24th 7:15 A.M.

We have met the enemy and he is us.

~ Pogo

"Lee, you've got to get up. Lord knows you need a shower."

"Okay, okay." Lee sat up and winced. "My head is killing me."

"Here are some aspirin." She placed two in his hand.

"Thanks." He rubbed his eyes. The pressure felt good.

"I hope I've gotten everything." She was on her knees looking under the bed. "I think so, but I can be so forgetful these days." Lee stumbled to the bathroom.

"Here are your—I mean Emanuel's—street clothes."

Lee put the clothes under his arm and closed the bathroom door.

Joann continued to talk, and Lee continued to grunt or offer an occasional "yes" or "uh-huh," at least until he stepped into the shower. As usual, the warm water felt healing. His head still ached, and his thoughts were scrambled, but he felt a bit better.

What was real? What wasn't? What would he tell Jennings? No, what would Jennings believe? Why should he waste his breath? Jennings wanted the package, not a story about aliens, ghost ships, hundred-year-old cab drivers, and friends returning from the dead. He'd just deliver the disk and tell Jennings that he was going to stop playing "I Spy." But was the package the same one he got in London? Griff had switched them, hadn't he? Lee wasn't even sure of that. He wished the whole thing was just a dream.

He was still developing his plan, if one could call it that, when Joann banged on the door.

"Lee, honey, come on!"

"Coming, coming." He quickly shaved and put on his street clothes: Slacks, a shirt, and a sportscoat. The tan was fading and more hair had fallen out. He stared into the mirror for a second. He was starting to look like his old, very old, self. He sighed and opened the door.

"You can go on. I'll check us out with the head steward."

Their eyes met. "I told Father Allen that I'd get you to Boston, and I've kept my word," said Joann.

"You were always good at doing that, unlike me." She smiled.

"How are you doing this morning?" asked Lee, apologetically, but the moment was gone.

"I'm just fine. And you?"

He paused. "Oh, I'm fine too." But he knew they weren't. "I appreciate you. I've . . ."

"Dr. Brazil, look at me. Be happy with the people and things you have now, and the memories that you'll always have."

She hugged him, and he kissed her on the forehead.

"Now go," she said, pushing him away.

Lee got to the door and turned. "I'll see you in Portland, when . . . well, whenever I get back."

"Maybe." She looked away. "I'll just check the bathroom one last time. Don't want to leave anything."

Lee took Emanuel's watch cap off a hook by the door and pulled it down to his ears then zipped up a heavy coat and put his hook in its pocket.

No one seemed to look or care as he left. The ship's officer glanced at him and his passport and waved him through to another line that was moving quickly. Most of the crew were leaving only for the day, and many would stay aboard over the holiday. They had only a carry-on bag at most.

His heart was pounding as he approached the customs officer. Slow, deep breaths helped, but his head ached, and he hoped to God he didn't have say anything in his broken Spanish.

Lee smiled at the officer, who ignored the gesture and focused on the passport. "Are you returning to your ship this evening?"

Lee nodded and muttered "*si*."

The officer looked up, smiled, winked, and allowed him to pass.

He knew where he was. Black Falcon Avenue, only a few blocks from Jennings' office. He pushed through sightseers. The sun was out, and even though the temperature was in the low forties, it was a beautiful day.

Lord, it's Christmas Eve, Lee thought. I didn't even wish Joann a Merry Christmas. Maybe when I get back. She did say maybe . . .

"Stop!" he said aloud and focused again on Jennings. He crossed the street. The crowd had thinned. His legs still felt like spaghetti, and walking on cobblestones didn't help. Don't turn your ankle, he warned himself. Watch where you're stepping. Slowly.

He stopped to re-tie his left shoe and noticed that a person a half block behind him also stopped. Yes, he was sure that he was being followed. He tried not to look back. Maybe he was wrong. He looked back again. The man was still there, approximately half a block away.

He was close to Jennings' office, so he increased his pace. His stalker appeared to do the same.

Lee turned left, as did the man. He was now only a block from Jennings' office. If this person wanted the package, he'd take it now. It would be his only chance. Lee pushed the disk down farther into his breast pocket and buttoned the top buttons of his coat.

When he reached Jennings' office, he was jogging. He climbed the steps two at a time and burst into the nondescript brick building that housed Jennings' office and the detention center. Most people weren't supposed to know that it was an FBI office building, and no one was supposed to know about the small detention center that had just a number over a door: 136.

He'd made it. Or had he? He looked to see what his stalker was doing. To Lee's surprise, the young, blond man in a black trench coat and sunglasses was coming up the steps. He opened the door, and Lee stepped back, holding his breath.

"Pardon me," the young man said, as he stepped past Lee and was buzzed into the building.

Lee exhaled and took a deep breath. "Lord," he said out loud, "what tricks your mind can play on you." He picked up the intercom phone.

"May I help you?" asked a woman's voice.

"Yes. I need to see Agent Jennings."

"Do you have an appointment?" "No."

"Your name?"

"Just tell him Dr. Brazil is here. I believe he'll want to see me."

The line went dead. Lee hung up and waited, but not for long. The door buzzed open and a young woman in full security gear beckoned him to come with her. They rode the elevator to the fourth floor.

When the door opened, she pointed to a security agent sitting at a desk. "Mr. Jones will help you."

Lee stepped off the elevator and stood in front of Mr. Jones' desk while he finished a phone conversation. "Got it?" Jones said. "Don't worry about it." He turned his attention to Lee. "Come with me."

He'd reached Boston. The relief brought by this realization made him almost giddy. He followed Jones down a long hall into a large room with at least a dozen cubicles. Most were empty for Christmas Eve. Finally, they reached the door of a small office that looked out on the bay. Jennings had his back to the door, focusing on his computer. Lee entered but said nothing. Jennings, hearing their approach, sprang to his feet.

"Come in, come in. Welcome to Boston," he said. "Can I get you something to drink? Maybe coffee?"

"Uh . . . sure," said Lee, a bit taken aback by the effusive welcome.

He finally noticed Jones waiting. "Oh, just cream, no sugar." Jones nodded and disappeared.

"Well, sit down," said Jennings, gesturing to a straight-back wooden chair in front of his desk. "You've had quite a trip through the Triangle."

"To say the least."

"No tales of lights in the sky, or Flight 19, or lost ships?" he asked, with an expression between a smile and a sneer."

Lee smiled but said nothing.

"Did you enjoy London and Paris? Paris is my favorite. But let's not talk about me; let's talk about what you've brought me."

Lee pulled the package from his breast pocket and laid it on the desk.

Jennings quickly began examining it. "Yes," he said, as he flipped it over.

"Looks like it's okay. The seals haven't been broken."

When Jones reentered the room with the coffee and handed it to Lee, Jennings gestured to him. "Here, Ben, take this out to George and ask. . . well, he'll know what to do." Then he refocused on Lee, "Not that I don't trust you and what you've told me, but we do need to scan it."

Lee raised his eyebrows. "I haven't told you anything."

"Exactly," said Jennings. "Why so quiet?"

"I doubt you'd really be that interested."

"Well, maybe not."

"I . . . I just hope," said Lee, uncertain of what to say to Jennings. "You . . . you..." You're not surprised that I'm here this morning."

"No, we were expecting you," said Jennings. "You lost us for about twenty-four hours, but we figured out where you were and were going."

Lee caught Jennings' eye. "You had some help doing that." The statement was a dig. Lee knew that the FBI hated relying on private security firms to do anything.

Jennings grimaced. "Oh, yes. Our friendly government contractor Hollocore. Their security folks were very helpful."

Jennings leaned forward. "Look, Dr. Brazil, I know things got a little dicey in Paris."

He might be trying his best to sound apologetic, but Lee continued to stare, adding, "And London and Bermuda."

"I know, but mistakes do happen. What's important is that you're here, the package is here, and it's Christmas Eve." Jennings smiled.

"I'm not doing this again," said Lee, standing.

"Exactly," agreed Jennings. "I wouldn't ask. But you know . . ."

"Skip the patriotic BS. I'm way too old to be running errands for you."

"Well, thank you," said Jennings, "for your service, Dr. Brazil."

Jones opened the door. "It all checks out."

"You can leave now. Jones will show you out." Jennings turned back around to face his computer.

Lee stood there for a moment, thinking about what he should say next. "I suppose I should tell you..."

Jennings showed no signs of interest in what Lee was saying.

"We must hurry, Dr. Brazil," said Jones. "We've arranged for your bags to come off a London flight into Logan. Your wife and daughter will meet that flight." Jones showed Lee to a car waiting at the loading dock at the back of the building.

It was Christmas Eve, and every bad driver who had miraculously survived another year in Boston was on the road. But the driver of the nondescript black Crown Vic, one of the last left in the FBI fleet—they loved that model—made amazing good time. On the way to Logan, Jones explained that they'd e-mailed Liz using his Qmail address and told her that he'd been delayed and had lost his cell phone, which was true.

Lee found himself thinking about Joann again, of the time that she'd driven all the way from Maine to Logan to pick him up when he missed his flight to Portland. And then he'd gotten them lost in godforsaken Swampscott at two o'clock in the morning, trying to get back to Maine.

He stopped himself again. He and Joann had established separate lives, and that was most likely how it would be forever. She'd always focused on what was in front of her at the moment. "Be happy with the people and the things that you have in your life now. You'll always have your memories" sounded like a line from *Casablanca,* but it was true, and it worked for her. "The present," she would say, "is the only thing that can give us hope for the future," and that was certainly true. Tonight *was* Christmas Eve.

At the airport, Jones helped Lee pick his way through the crowd and move through security quickly. He handed Lee a baggage claim slip and a cancelled ticket and left.

It took a few minutes, but Lee found Liz in the crowd. He hugged her tightly and said nothing.

"You're okay," she said. "I was so worried." She'd been crying. "More this time than when you were in Boston. I thought . . ."

"I'm okay. A little sore and bruised for the wear and tear, but okay." Tears were welling in his own eyes.

"Do you think your bag will make it? The one I loaned you?" asked Liz. "I checked the 'thing.' Had to pay extra this time for the weight. You've got to get rid of that thing."

"Well, we missed a perfect opportunity." "What do you mean?" asked Liz.

"You know, Heathrow loses a lot of luggage."

"But I really like the bag I loaned you," Liz persisted. "I hope . . ."

"I know, I know . . ."

"And where'd you get all the new clothes . . . and the tan?

"Emanuel's," said Lee. "You like?" "Huh? Never heard of it."

"And a long walk on a sunny day for the tan."

Liz raised her eyebrows. She seemed most puzzled by Lee's hair, even though much of the new growth had fallen out.

"What did you do to your hair? Are you using that hair growth stuff? I warned you about the chemicals in that."

"I know, I know. We'll talk about it later."

"Dru and her fiancé are somewhere." Liz scanned the crowd. "She texted me." She lowered her voice conspiratorially. "They plan on getting married in the spring, and they're talking about having a family." She paused "But don't say I told you. She wants to talk with you about it." She scanned the baggage claim area again. "They have a nice room for us at the Westin. We'll do Christmas at their apartment in the morning."

"That's wonderful," said Lee. "Hope springs eternal, especially on Christmas Eve."

Lee saw his bag and started for it. Liz followed.

"So, what happened? Why were you delayed?" "It's a long story, and you wouldn't believe me if I told you." "Try me," said Liz with determination.

Lee smiled warmly. "Okay. But if I tell you, I'll have to . . ."
They both laughed.

CHAPTER 33

Executive Offices of TransSea
Hamilton, Bermuda
Monday, December 27th, 10:45 A.M.

God will delight when we are creators of
justice and joy, compassion and peace. For
everyone born, a place at the table.

~ JOY F. PATTERSON & SHIRLEY ERENA MURRAY
For Everyone Born
(A Place at the Table)

"Come in, Philip. I am glad that you could be here on such short notice. I wanted to talk with you for a few minutes before we meet with our visitor from Home Office."

Philip Perkins took a seat across from his colleague Bradford Jenkins at a small table in the TransSea conference room. Jenkins wasn't much older than Perkins, but he'd moved up quickly through the ranks at TransSea and had been stationed in Bermuda longer.

Jenkins' friends at Home admired him for taking the Bermuda assignment. They considered it dangerous, and it was. They kidded him about wanting to save the world. It had taken over a year to convince the company to place him in Bermuda. He wanted to be here. He wanted to make a difference. To change the world and, yes, maybe even save it.

He was a good communicator. He was also well liked, flexible, and took good care of himself and his employees. Perhaps most of all, he was an optimist. He believed that few things, good or bad, last forever and that few events can change everything one way or the other. He also believed in treating others justly, with mercy—values that he had learned as a child back Home. He was aware that his community had taken a long time to master them. But he had patience.

"Is this about our unfortunate Mr. Jefferson Davis Powell?"

"No, no. Mr. Powell served his purpose well, I think; would you agree? And Dr. Brazil is all right. He just has what they call a 'hangover.'"

"Yes, I think that Mr. Powell did a marvelous job. He certainly helped convince Hollocore that our company wanted Dr. Brazil's package."

"Hollocore security will release him in a few days. In the meantime, I wired his wife some additional funds, given their situation."

Perkins nodded. "Even if Mr. Powell *had* obtained the package, Hollocore security would have taken it from him before *The Saint* docked in Boston. Either way would have worked in our favor."

"I am pleased with our sector. Our London associates performed well, staging that near miss at the airport with Dr. Brazil . . ."

"And the lorry and taxi. Driving motorized vehicles in that way certainly requires skill, does it not?"

Jenkins nodded. "I want to commend you and your staff, as well. The rope ladder, and the he helicopter billowing black smoke on cue. Brilliant."

"Thank you. David also played his role well. I hear he always does."

"Yes. We achieved the company's objective. Hollocore believes that we made every effort but failed to prevent the package from falling into their hands. They believe that they have the 'real deal,' as they say here. Instead, they have a disk with a number of viruses."

Perkins smiled. "A disk that should misdirect and confuse them for quite some time." He paused, frowning. "I am somewhat disappointed, however, with our failure to have Mr. Bowman meet with Dr. Brazil at the White's Ferry cottage."

"You are not at fault. Leaking propane tanks." He shook his head. "Humans can be so careless. At least you were able to abort the meeting."

"Yes, but, unfortunately, we arrived too late to prevent the explosion."

"As long as no one was hurt," Jenkins reminded him then leaned forward. "I also want to tell you of my communication with Home Office this morning. They asked that we provide our new assistant with all that he requires. They informed me that he has specifically requested to visit the abandoned USA Army base. He believes it to be an excellent location to receive and transmit electronic transmissions. You and your team have responsibility for the security of that area. What is there that would be useful to him?"

"I am unsure. It does have very old communication towers. We also store drilling rigs in dry dock there and have warehouses of old communication equipment and transformers that the company has used in other sectors to receive and redirect energy transmissions. I suppose that we could help our assistant Jerry Wig something."

"Gerry-rig," Jenkins corrected. They both smiled.

"Unlike the two of us, our assistant has been working undercover for the company in this sector for a very long time," said Jenkins.

"I must ask how long it took him to acclimate to this climate."

They both loved the warm weather, especially the gentle fall breezes that reminded them of the prevailing warm winds of Home. But the hurricanes were frightening, and, with global warming, they knew that more would occur. Most difficult about the climate were the increasing levels of CO_2 and other airborne pollutants that affected their breathing, especially Philip's. Most of the pollution was not created by Bermuda but came from the coal-fired energy plants that still operated with little regulation in the United States. Some days were worse than others. Visiting Home was a relief but returning to Bermuda meant readapting.

'I know that when I visit Home and return, the process starts over."

Perkins grimaced. "That is not good news."

Jenkins sighed. "Home is so different from Bermuda, isn't it, Philip?" Perkins nodded.

"The change is always disorienting to me. And I loathe being separated from my children." His two children lived with his ex-partner, a successful engineer from whom he had separated long ago. Their community was supportive and expected them to raise their offspring well and to meet their responsibilities to them and their community first. The society was not free of problems, but it resolved them. Differences and conflicts were not its main focus. Everyone could voice an opinion, but compromise was the expectation, not the exception.

"I miss Home; do you?" "I do," Perkins agreed.

"The most difficult aspect of this assignment is the isolation—feeling that we do not belong."

Philip smiled. "And we do not."

Jenkins ignored the comment. "Did I tell you of the two women in the market?"

"No."

"I attempted to converse with them about a grapefruit." Philip smiled.

"I do not know what I said or did, but when they thought that I could not hear them, one said, 'He is not from around here.'"

Indeed, he attempted to assimilate. In general, however, he did not share the values of most people he met. These differences troubled him; his personal mission on assignments was always to become part of the communities in which he worked. But status and the acquisition of wealth were not important to him, or to most of those in the community in which he had grown up and now lived.

"I do not find the local people so very different from us. Rather, the disparities become most evident when we work and socialize with those employed by mega-corporations."

"I feel similarly," Perkins agreed, "but I do not allow the differences to bother me. I remain focused. Those *are* the people who control this world's economy. Those *are* the people with whom we must work."

"I know, and I agree, Philip. But I do not have to like it."

Philip Perkins took a different approach to his assignment in Bermuda.

"Bradford, you and I are quite different in many ways. I do not share your interest in assimilating. I have become tired of telling people the false story of my life that the company created for me: "I am from a small farming community in South Africa," he droned.

Philip had neither a partner nor offspring. And he hadn't been in Bermuda as long but performed his job adequately; Bradford had no complaints about that. But he didn't have the same drive or passion.

"Philip, perhaps you would feel differently if you became more involved with the community. We can make a difference here, you know."

Like Bradford, Philip was a good communicator and had worked in other sectors as a mediator. But, unlike Bradford, he was not hopeful about the company's mission in Bermuda.

"As I have said before, I believe that the company has waited too long. The forces that we are attempting to check and contain are very strong and well established."

Bradford nodded in agreement.

"That said, you know that I will support you and the company and, to the best of my ability, thwart the efforts of organizations like Hollocore. But as you also know, I do not share your optimism regarding the outcome."

TransSea understood that mega-corporations—especially energy companies—not the governments of the world, were now in control. If significant change was to occur, it would be through these corporations. For TransSea to show them a way to win other than through creating, at any cost, the largest dividends for their investors, they first would have to first "beat them at their own game." That, not profit, was TransSea's main objective. As a privately held corporation, it was not accountable to shareholders and certainly had the resources and talent to compete with organizations like Hollocore. TransSea was recognized for its work, but dealing with a creature like Chambers, who wanted to best his competitors, was something new for the company.

Home Office had a plan, however. They had worried about Hollocore for some time, as Bradford and Philip believed they should. Exactly what Home Office was planning, they did not know. Their work with Mr. Powell and Dr. Brazil was part of the plan, but something much bigger was afoot. Hopefully, they would learn what from their new assistant.

"The bottom line—I do like that expression—is that our assistant will be in charge of implementing the company's plans for the Beta 17 project."

"Perhaps we could find our unfortunate Mr. Powell a job on Beta 17."

"Perhaps. We will discuss that."

The intercom buzzed. "Yes, Judy?"

"Mr. Jenkins, are you expecting someone?"

"Yes, yes. Please show him in."

The door to the conference room opened, and both men stood.

"Come in, sir. I am Bradford Jenkins and this is Philip Perkins.

Their visitor, a handsome young man with short blond hair and bright green eyes, extended his hand. "I am Edward Zan."

CHAPTER 34

Maine Turnpike
30 Miles South of Bangor, Maine
Thursday, December 30th, 2:27 P.M.

L iz and Lee had gotten a late start north. Eastport was at least four hours from Winterpool, and with the roads as bad as they were, the going would be slow. It had finally snowed on Christmas Day, and then it hadn't stopped. They had two feet on the ground in most places.

The pilgrimage to Eastport had become a tradition for the family and for Mike and June. They usually drove up together the day before New Year's Eve, but this year, Mike, the Fire Chief of Winterpool, was tied up with some end-of-the-year fire department business. They would join them the next day. And Dru and her boyfriend wouldn't be up either until that afternoon. So, it was just Lee and Liz.

Driving to Bangor in the late-afternoon winter sun was relaxing, but as the light faded and the wind picked up, the driving became anything but. And the sun was gone by four o'clock.

The Festival of Lights would soon end. The last day of Hanukkah would be on New Year's Eve. As last night's candles had burned down and flickered out, they'd both felt a strange sense of foreboding. Now, as the winter darkness gathered in and around them, they felt it again.

They took turns at the wheel. Liz read or thumbed through a magazine when not driving, but as it got darker, she decided to try the radio.

"What's wrong with this thing? When are you getting rid of this car?"

"In a couple of years. . . and there's nothing wrong with the radio."

"Well, what's going on with it?" She ran the scanner across the channels. Only static.

"The same thing that's going on with the cell phones and the Internet. They say it's because of increased solar activity, although I read in the *Almanac* that solar activity was supposed to *decrease* in the next few years."

Liz finally gave up and turned the radio off.

"They say it's getting worse. It was on the front page of the paper this morning," Lee volunteered. "If this keeps up, newspapers may make a comeback." He smiled; he'd certainly like that.

"What else could be causing it?" Liz asked, with concern.

"I don't really know. If you read the Internet—when it's up—you can take your pick. Secret military experiments gone awry, aliens, who knows."

"Ooo . . . okay," said Liz. "I guess I'll take increased solar activity."

Conversation faded as Lee concentrated on his driving.

Lee and Liz hadn't talked much during the previous week. Lee had refused to talk about his time in Paris, and when Liz had asked questions, he'd been evasive.

Lee thought she'd finally given up. He knew that she noticed him spending most of his time on the Internet—when it worked—reading about UFO sightings and alien encounters. She'd even voiced how strange all this was, even for him. But he knew what she felt was the strongest change: his lack of reaction to the news that his only daughter was getting married. He couldn't explain his failure to react. He felt happy for her but couldn't express it. He didn't know why.

He'd anticipated that Liz might bring all this up again on the drive north, but the difficult driving had produced enough tension between them. He was relieved that she apparently didn't want to discuss something that would only create more.

They stopped in Machias for supper at Helen's, a mom-and-pop diner that had been there for God knows how long. It had burned down once but they'd rebuilt. The food was good, but the pies were out of this world. As Liz would say, the strawberry pie was "to die for."

From the diner, they called Winton House, the bed and breakfast where they would be staying, and explained that they would be later than planned.

"No problem," said the owner, Jane Giroux. "Just drive safe." Lee had always thought that Jane's face should be on boxes of breakfast cereal, like 'Heartland-Good For You In Every Way Organic Oatmeal.' Just a couple of years older than them, Jane mothered them just like she mothered everyone else.

She and her husband Bill were waiting up when Liz and Lee finally arrived. Bill was ready with a small glass of sherry.

"Cold night," he said. "A small nip on a night like this is good for the circulation."

Lee agreed and didn't refuse the offer. Maybe he should have, but he told himself he didn't want to hurt Bill's feelings.

The bed and breakfast was small, just four guestrooms and two shared baths. Fireplaces in each room. They had converted two of them to house wood stoves. The house was filled with antiques that Jane had collected over the years. An "eclectic mix," as Liz referred to it. She liked Jane and her taste.

As Jane and Liz caught up, Lee and Bill hauled the luggage up to the same room they'd had for the last four years. A warm, dark green, it had one of the wood stoves, but Liz would still complain about being cold. They would just add more covers to the pile of blankets and quilts already on the large Queen Anne bed. The room also had a small writing desk, two or three chairs—one was comfortable—and a TV that didn't work most of the time.

"You know," said Bill, "we bought this place forty-five years ago, at least it will be forty-five this summer." Bill surveyed the room. "I'd just been discharged from the Navy after two tours in 'Nam." He straightened one of the wildlife paintings. "I really needed to get away from everything."

"I would assume that Eastport has been the right place for that."

"Oh, yes." Billed smiled. "Fixing up an old sea captain's home in America's Easternmost City was very good therapy. It occupied both mind and hands. And when we got the house in the seventies, it was a bargain. The property values were dropping, but so were prices."

Downstairs, Liz was admiring a new painting of Eastport that Jane had purchased from a local artist.

"Eastport was an active deep-water port in its day," Jane offered. "But by the early eighties, much of the shipping had moved to ports farther south, and many of the sardine canneries that had employed so many closed. The few canneries that remained closed in the nineties. Unemployment increased, and the population shrank to fourteen hundred by 2010."

"I assume that this painting was created from a photograph taken sometime after World War II?" asked Liz.

"Yes. It was a busy place in those days." She sighed. "But Eastport began to lose ground in the late forties and early fifties. When the military left, the money left." Jane changed the subject.

"What brings you folks back every year to our little part of the world?"

"Lee and I were talking about that on the way up," Liz replied. "It's the spirit of the county, I guess. Aroostook is one of the largest but least populated counties in the state."

"In the nation," Jane added.

"We love that people know and seem to take care of each other. And nothing reflects that better, at least for us, than what you folks do on New Year's Eve."

Jane smiled. Townspeople had begun 'dropping' an eight-foot wooden sardine about thirty years ago. A few years later, they'd added the maple leaf drop at 11:00 p.m. Eastern Standard Time, midnight Atlantic Time, to symbolize the close relationship between the peoples of Eastport and Canada, which many residents could literally see from their front porch.

"Most people think that the sardine is just a symbol of Eastport's past, when it was a thriving port and factory town. But it's more than that." "Is CNN covering it again this year?" asked Liz.

"Yes, and I assume that they'll miss the main point yet again."

"So, what is the main point, as you see it, Lee?"

"The real story is of a community that's had hard times for a while but comes together with pride and hope for the future each New Year's Eve."

"And if you kiss the sardine on the lips, you'll have good luck in the next year." Liz chuckled.

"That's what they say," agreed Jane, "but I don't know. That hasn't always worked for me."

It was late, so Liz excused herself, but Lee wasn't ready for bed. Traditionally, he and Bill had a pre-New Year's drink. Just one. Usually a brandy.

He found Bill in the living room, waiting, glasses already filled. They talked about the year. Eastport was pretty much the same, and Bill was grateful that and his wife still had their health. Lee wanted to talk about the strangeness of last few weeks but didn't know how. He could see that Bill was fading and ready for the night to end, but, before he could make his exit, another guest hurried in. He made his apologies for the late hour and asked if he could make a Jack Daniels Manhattan on the rocks. Being a good host, Bill couldn't refuse.

Lee nodded but didn't speak. He hadn't seen the man before. He was an average looking fellow, late or mid fifties Lee guested. He seemed a bit anxious. While Bill made the drink, he wandered around the living room looking at the photographs of Eastport that lined the walls.

"Here's your drink, Mr. Black."

"Lou will do."

"Well, Lou, I'm going to take my leave; It's been a long day. If you and Doc want another one, just help yourself and put it on your tab."

"Lee Brazil." He extended his hand; Lou took it and said down on the barstool next to him.

"Brazil? You're the psychologist from Winterpool who was in the papers a few years ago."

Lee could feel his face flush as he nodded.

"Got into trouble with the government. Got bombed on your taxes."

Lee started to say something in his defense, but suddenly wondered how this man knew anything about his IRS problem. He looked again at Lou. He recognized him.

"Black," he said, "the accountant with Hayes, Edwards and . . ."

"The glorified bookkeeper with Hayes, Edwards and Peabody."

"You helped me work out that mess with the IRS."

"So, you're square with the feds?" asked Lou.

"Well, not with everything." God knows that was true. "But it's a very long story."

Lou smiled and nodded.

"You still working for Hayes, Edwards and . . ."

"Peabody? No, and that's a very long story, too."

They both laughed.

"So," asked Lee, "have you been to Eastport before?"

"No. First time. You?"

"Oh, yeah. We've been doing this for a lot of years. A family tradition."

"I know what you mean. The ex-wife and our kids used to go to First Night in Portland. Did that for a lot of years."

"You're divorced?" Lee asked.

"Yeah. A couple of years ago. We were married for a lot of years. But the last few . . . well, you know. I left then tried to come back, but she was done. Can't blame her. I gave up on the marriage. We went to marriage counseling, but it was too late by the time I finally got around to taking it seriously. I think I never felt what I should have after all those years."

Lee just nodded, somewhat taken aback by the man's chattiness.

Whatever happened to small talk, he wondered, and tried to engage in some. "Are you here by yourself, then?"

"No, no; I'm with an old girlfriend. A good woman. We've talked about getting married but never have. She's been single a long time, and I don't know if she wants to take on me, my ex-wife, and our two girls. Plus, the girls blame me and her for the divorce, and they probably should."

"Not feeling the way you should is a tough one," said Lee.

"How do you mean?" asked Lou.

"Well, people and feelings change over time. Love changes. Sometimes, you just have to accept what you have and be grateful for it."

"That sounds like settling and giving up to me," said Lou.

"No, I think acceptance and gratitude are a bit different from that."

Lou didn't respond.

"Well, some of that may have to do with my age. Age can help with acceptance and gratitude." Lee chuckled. "But I do think that you can either focus on what you don't have with your partner or what you do. It's your choice."

"I guess I should think about that," said Lou, in a voice that made Lee think he would.

They finished their drinks and said their goodnights.

Lee lingered by the fireplace and watched the flickering embers as the fire died away. He thought a lot about what he'd said and the choices he'd made. He and Lou had made different choices. Lee had stayed; Lou hadn't. Lee realized that he finally felt satisfied with what he'd chosen. He hoped that Lou felt the same.

Lee and Lou slept late . . .well, as late as they could without missing breakfast. Winton House was known for its "full breakfast." This morning, it was New Orleans-style French toast, Cajun sausage, and wonderful coffee. Lee loved the coffee.

Still too early for shopping, they drove to Ray's mustard factory for their annual tour and tasting. Eastport was home to the only stone-ground mustard factory left in the United States. Their tour guide, a local woman whom they'd seen on previous tours, explained proudly that Eastport had been making mustard since the turn of the twentieth century. The factory proudly displayed its national and international awards and blue ribbons in a trophy case.

"The mustard was used first in the canning of sardines. Ray's still uses the original equipment and millstones," she pointed to them, "that this factory installed when it was built in 1903." Last of all, she said with pride, "It's a flavor that modern technology has left behind."

Lee had heard her say this before, but it had a different meaning for him today. Perhaps modern technology has left a lot more behind than just the flavor of mustard, he thought.

Lee and Liz finally arrived on Water Street, Eastport's main street. Public Works plows were busy with snow removal. Most of the shops were just opening. After making her initial rounds, with Lee in tow, Liz was ready for something else. She'd read in the local paper that morning about the Passamaquoddy's weeklong forgiveness ceremony for the New Year at the reservation's Community Center. In it, the People of the Dawn, as they called themselves, asked forgiveness from other community members and humbled themselves before the animals and spirits of the forest. Lee found it odd that a native people should be asking for forgiveness. given the treatment they'd received at the hands of nonnative peoples.

The village was only a few miles from Eastport. They arrived as the afternoon ceremony was beginning. The director of the center addressed the forty or so people in attendance. "This year," she explained, "our elders were told in a dream to extend this ceremony to a week and open it to all people. In addition to much drumming and dancing, we will have prayers and singing in our language, which I will interpret as best I can."

Toward the ceremony's conclusion, she said, "We believe that something very important is about to happen. The people of our world must approach this event with humility."

When questioned about this declaration, she became more emotional and finally left the room. The tribe members who remained seemed even less willing to answer questions.

The sun was setting as Lee and Liz drove back to Eastport.

"What do you think she was referring to?"

"I don't know, but I have a similar feeling."

Liz didn't ask what he meant, which was not her nature, and Lee didn't volunteer more, which *was* his.

When they arrived back at Winton House, it was almost four-thirty. They decided to take a short nap before dinner, but Lee couldn't sleep. He smiled, thinking about the old mill and the flavor that modern technology had left behind. But mostly, he thought about the People of the Dawn. They were concerned that something important was about to happen to the world and that humanity must approach it with humility and ask for forgiveness.

They were up at seven. They had reservations at the Happy Clam for eight o'clock. June and Mike would meet them there. They decided to take the car, which was definitely a mistake.

United Flight 4502
Portland Air Space, Portland, Maine
Friday, December 31st, 7:38 P.M. EST

The night was clear and cold. In the crisp air, the stars appeared like cut glass, close enough to touch.

"This is your Captain speaking. We are making our final approach. We should be on the ground in Portland in approximately fifteen minutes."

Captain Art Rogers clicked off the intercom and turned to his First Officer, Jeff Standish.

"So, what are you doing for New Year's Eve, Jeff?"

Jeff smiled. "Spending it with you, unless the company has other ideas."

As always, New Year's Eve being no exception, they would do a quick turnaround in Portland and fly back to Chicago, arriving at O'Hare a few minutes before eleven Central Time. Art Rogers had been flying for twenty-five years, and First Officer Standish for fifteen. They moved meticulously through their checklists, their steady hands passing silently over the cockpit instrument console.

"What a night," said Standish. "Visibility is unbelievable."

Indeed, they could see Portland Headlight's beacon off the aircraft's right wing. The lights of Biddeford and Saco were directly below them, Portland Harbor and the city to the northeast.

Their attention was suddenly diverted from checklists and instruments. They both saw it, directly in their flightpath. A bright blue light.

Standish called in. "Portland tower, this is Flight 4502. Please confirm that we are the only flight on this approach."

"Roger. Confirm Flight 4502. You are the only show in town. Nothing else on your approach or our screen."

"We have a visual, an unidentified, about ten miles out, closing fast."

"Repeat, Flight 4502. You're breaking up . . . Go ahead, 4502."

As the flight controller continued to speak, a very bright circular object streaked silently past the cockpit, only a few hundred feet above the plane.

"What the hell was that, Art?"

"Portland Control, did you see that?" asked Rogers, his voice climbing. "Whatever it was . . . just . . . just missed us."

"This is Portland Control. Flight 4502, we have nothing in your area on our screen. Do you wish to make a report?"

The pilots were silent.

"Flight 4502, do you wish to make a report?"

Captain Rogers responded. "Negative, Portland Control.

We'll pass."

The two men silently resumed their final checks before landing. Both had seen other strange lights in the night sky, and they'd learned that the less said, the better. They'd done the paperwork and tried to answer the questions that came with reporting a sighting. Once had been enough.

CHAPTER 35

Eastport, Maine
Friday, December 31st, 7:34 P.M.

*Do good . . . be rich in good works, generous and ready to
share . . .so that you may take hold of the life that really is life.*

~ 1 TIMOTHY 6:18-19

"There's a parking spot over there, Lee. Lee . . . Lee!" "Do
you want to drive, Liz? If you do, I'll pull over and let you,"
he said, raising his voice.

"I was trying to . . ." she sounded exasperated. "There's one
right there.

Between those two cars."

"Okay, okay." Lee stopped the car and started to back up. Parallel
parking had become more difficult because of the arthritis in his neck.

"I don't know if you're . . . going to make it," said Liz,
sounding anxious.

"I won't if you continue to try and help me." Lee was starting
to flush.

He pulled the car out and tried again. This time Liz restrained
herself, and

Lee managed to maneuver his old Subaru into the space. He
sighed with relief and turned off the engine.

Liz's cell phone buzzed. She answered it.

"Sure, honey, we'll meet you and Rob in front of the museum.
We just got here. You know your father. He had to find the right
parking space."

Lee grimaced.

"Okay, okay. See you soon." She hung up. "Mike and June are going to meet us at the restaurant, Lee?"

"Yeah, he's the smart one. He and June are walking over from the inn."

"We could have walked." She bent over and tried to make eye contact, but Lee resisted. "I didn't say no."

"I know, I know. It's all right." Lee finally looked at her. "I know your knee has been bothering you." "Not that much," she protested.

"Well, be that as it is or may. We're here."

The restaurant was near the end of Water Street. It had a good view of the harbor, as did each of the four restaurants on the street. Locals in the know had reserved tables on the harbor side, but Liz and Lee's table wasn't the greatest; it was near the door. Normally, Liz would complain about being cold, but she wasn't, which surprised Lee. Maybe she knew it wouldn't do much good: every table was taken.

Mike and June were late. "Sorry," said Mike. "I went by the fire station to get Bobby. Bobby Sanford, meet Dr. Brazil and his wife Liz."

Bobby extended his hand and Lee shook it. He looked to be in his early twenties: red hair and a little overweight, with a bad case of acne.

"Have a seat, guys," said Lee. "This was the best table we could get." He'd called late; in fact, he almost hadn't called at all. He'd thought about cancelling the whole trip, but tradition was important to him, even when things had been as crazy as they'd been in the last few weeks.

"You're welcome to join us, Bob. We have a couple of extra places. My daughter and her fiancé won't be here for a couple of hours."

The waiter came and took their orders. Everyone ordered seafood: two fried clams; one scallop; one haddock; and one Maine shrimp, the specialty of the house. A bottle of champagne came with dinner, and Mike quickly opened it and started serving.

"So, you're a fireman?" asked Liz.

"Trainee. The Chief helped me get the job." A dispatch call interrupted the conversation. "Excuse me," he said and bounded out the door.

Sitting by the door had perks, Lee mused. "Seems like a nice kid."

Mike nodded. The waiter brought the drinks.

"Things are really busy tonight . . . and crazy," said Mike.

"Tell me about it," groaned Lee. "They have been for the last few weeks." Mike looked at Lee. "People have been seeing more of these crazy lights in the sky the last few weeks. And tonight, they're all over the place. I bet the call Bobby got from dispatch is another one."

"So, what's going on?" asked Lee. "You're the expert on this stuff." Mike was known in Winterpool for his interest in space and astronomy.

"You've got me. Like most people, I've always dismissed this hooey about UFOs. But that business at White's Bridge a couple of weeks ago . . . I don't know. And all these sightings in the last few days and tonight."

At that moment, Bobby burst in. "Chief, you should have seen it! A guy who lives in the apartment over the Pickled Cod, you know, the restaurant around the corner, has a telescope." Bobby was trying to tell the story and catch his breath at the same time. "He's been watching the tidal-wave power station a couple miles out in the harbor."

The station was a new success story for Eastport. The University in Orono and a private company had placed tidal-wave turbines on the bottom of the bay. that were beginning to generate most of the power needed by Eastport and some of the surrounding towns. They were even able to sell some of the excess power to the Canadian power grid.

Bobby continued. "He's been seeing these bright lights around the station all night. At first, he thought they were searchlights from a ship near the station, but these lights have been zipping around the station. He showed me. They were so bright, I couldn't see what they were. I was looking at them, and they just took off! I checked with the tech at the University monitoring the station. The station is unmanned. But she says that everything is fine. Nothing we should do, is there, Chief?"

"Just make a report of what you were told and saw and did."

"Yes, sir. That's what I'll do." He left, presumably to do just that.

Lee broached the topic on everyone's mind. "So maybe we're being visited by . . . aliens. For some reason, tonight they have an interest in the tidal-wave power station and apparently a lot of other things. Why is it so difficult to believe that other worlds like ours might exist, that our universe might hold other life forms? Perhaps these life forms are a good deal smarter than we are."

"Oh, Lee. Do you have to talk about this again? That's all you've been interested in talking about since you got back from our trip."

June spoke up. "Well, it gives me the creeps."

"Sorry," said Lee. "I don't want to creep you out, but I think you just answered part of my question." He'd learned early in his work to never underestimate people's ability to avoid and deny the existence of something they didn't understand and of which they were frightened.

"June's right. We can't get our heads around it. It scares us," said Mike.

"But, Mike, isn't this the decade of the commercial space age? TransSea recently unveiled elaborate plans to mine precious metals on asteroids in our solar system. Didn't they launch a robotic mining unit that will be landing on that large asteroid that's scheduled to pass close to Earth next week?"

"Yes. Beta-17," said Mike. "Economics spurred exploration on Earth. It will fuel space exploration."

"And possible exploitation," added Liz.

"Well, I think that we still see ourselves as being alone and at the center of the universe. Maybe we aren't. Maybe we have neighbors who are concerned about what we are doing."

Lee stopped himself. He felt like he was lecturing his friends, and he didn't like that. Maybe he should be talking to himself. He certainly felt like he'd become more self-obsessed since his almost retirement. Of course, self-centeredness is part of the human condition, but, hopefully, most people grow out of it at some point in their lives. He thought he had, but his colleague Dr. Wagner had certainly been able to pull up feelings that

Lee believed he'd addressed. His anger and cynicism seemed stronger tonight than they'd been in a long time. And all of this other stuff that was going on just confused him more as he thought about it. He didn't feel like talking anymore. The place was getting noisy, making conversation difficult.

The waiter finally came with their orders. The seafood was a great distraction. Lee had ordered the haddock, which he remembered was always prepared with lemon and garlic, just the way he liked it.

Bobby had returned, but before dinner ended, he was called out again. A fire alarm had gone off in a building downtown, but they couldn't find a fire. The power flickered a couple of times during dinner, and Mike explained that sometimes power surges set off alarms.

Condominium of Joann Lawrence
Portland, Maine
Friday, December 31st, 7:10 P.M.

Joann had spent part of Christmas Eve in Boston. She'd had a nice lunch at one of her favorite restaurants and shopped until the stores started to close. She'd picked up her rental and arrived back in Portland late in the evening. She had taken a quick look at her mail, taken a hot shower and went to bed. She slept late on

Christmas morning, visited with friends in the afternoon and had dinner with an old girlfriend.

The days before New Year's Eve had passed slowly for her. She was bored with Portland and thought about flying back to Palm Springs early. She was glad when New Year's Eve finally came; in another day, all the hoopla associated with the holidays would be over.

She decided to stay in and turned down an invitation from old friends to go out. She didn't like cooking and had never been good at it, so she opted for a nice Caesar salad. She'd even bought a small bottle of champagne.

She spent the early part of the evening rereading an old James Patterson novel; skipping the evening news, she didn't turn on the television until 11:40. She enjoyed watching the people in Times Square.

CHAPTER 36

Presidential Reception
White House
Washington, DC
Friday, December 31st, 8:30 P.M.

> *There must be virtue in frailty, for man is*
> *frail and man is a creation of God.*

> **~ KURT VONNEGUT,**
> *Player Piano*

P resident Bryant was entertaining. He was most comfortable hosting pig roasts at his Texas ranch and conducting government business at a dinner table with friends. Bryant, who'd run as a Republican, hadn't been favored but managed to win the 2024 election after a scandal came to light in the closing days of the campaign involving the Democratic nominee's husband's extramarital affair with a Russian ambassador's wife.

To say the least, the public, even Bryant himself, was surprised—some would say stunned—by the election results. Apparently, the Russians, as they had with Trump, had assisted his campaign, although an investigation uncovered no solid proof of collusion. In the 2026 midterm elections, his party lost seats in both the House and Senate and control of the House. This upset was enough to allow Democrats to block his efforts to promote what he and his base called "a populist agenda," which favored repealing healthcare legislation passed by Obama and rolling back more environmental regulations, gutting the latter primarily through executive orders.

Bryant prided himself on not being a politician but a successful businessman, a billionaire, the second one to hold the presidency. Also like the same predecessor, no one had ever seen his tax returns. He had no particularly strong opinions but was very responsive to his base, the people who'd elected him: predominantly right-wing, white American men. Party members soon learned that they couldn't control him, although he could easily be swayed, especially if doing so benefited him and his ego. Many considered him a narcissist; an equal number worried about him plunging the world into World War III. In so many ways, his tenure seemed like a rerun of a previous presidency. He continued the country's long and painful slide into authoritarianism.

In the three years he'd been in office, the Middle East had continued to simmer, but the economy had slowly improved, due largely to the actions of Obama and not the tax cut that the previous president had championed—the one that was now increasing the deficit well beyond the most pessimistic projections.

Conflicts with Iran and North Korea had also continued, as had mass shootings, many in schools, despite major efforts to change gun laws, especially in states with very liberal laws, which was a long list. Congress had made some progress in passing gun legislation after mass demonstrations by young people, but not enough. Bryant's agenda hadn't succeeded, but neither had the other parties'. Laws placed some restrictions on the sale of AR15s, but most people could still buy them at friendly neighborhood gun stores.

Like George W. and Trump, President Bryant was infamous for long vacations, but not to a ranch. He spent his time at Godfrey's, a golf resort that he owned in Palm Springs.

At the moment, President Bryant was trying to finish a conversation with one of his financial backers when Chief of Staff Jim Ramsey, a retired general, entered the room and moved quickly through the crowd to the President.

"Mr. President, may I speak with you?"

"You may," responded the President, "if these kind people will excuse me." They smiled and nodded, and the President followed his Chief of Staff into a private office. Ramsey closed the door.

"Thank God, you saved me from that conversation."

"Mr. President . . ."

"The stories I could tell you about that guy."

"Mr. President . . ."

"Mr. Chief of Staff. I was composing a tweet. That SOB from Tennessee, he supposedly retired from politics, but he . . ."

"Mr. President . . ."

"For Christ's sake, what is it, Jim?"

"General Mitchell is here. He needs to speak with you."

"Right now?" the President complained. "It's bad enough I have to spend the holiday in Washington. If Congress could make up its mind about what it's doing, I could get out of this God-forsaken town."

"He says it's urgent. I put him in your office."

"Okay, okay. Let's get this over with."

They walked down the hall to the West Wing, "What's Air & Space Command upset about now? Those damned lights in the sky that no one can explain? If he's going to talk to me again about alien life forms . . . my people aren't ready for that, and neither am I."

As they entered the Oval Office, General Mitchell rose and extended his hand. The President quickly shook his hand and smiled.

"So, what brings you to see me on New Year's Eve?"

Obviously, General Mitchell had important news, but equally obvious was that he didn't know how to present it to the President.

"Um, as you know, we've been observing the asteroid Beta-17, which has been drawing closer to Earth over the past few months."

Ramsey was quite sure that the President didn't know. He'd never bothered to read the briefing report, not even the summary.

"My staff now believes that it is the source of the electromagnetic storms that have been causing disruptions in our communication systems."

"You mean the phone, TV, and Internet? Yes, all of those connections have been lousy. I missed a *Fox & Friends* show last week because of it. Wait . . . are you saying that I won't be able to tweet?"

Ramsey could see that Mitchell was nearly ready to lose his patience with the President.

"Please, go on, General," he said in a voice tinged with apology. "Tonight we've seen an increase in electrical activity from Beta-17, which may be connected to many of the sightings across the globe during the last twenty- four hours."

"Sightings of what?" the President chuckled, but Mitchell didn't respond.

"Oh Lord, Mark, you came all the way over here to tell me this? As I told Ramsey, the American people aren't ready to hear about ET, and neither am I."

"Mr. President," Ramsey tried again, "the British and Europeans are taking this pretty seriously."

"Well . . . then let them deal with it." The President walked over to the window. After a moment or two, he turned. "Gentlemen, if it will make the two of you happy, move up the alert status."

The President walked to the door and looked back. "You haven't caught one of those little fellas, have you?"

Mitchell turned to avoid Bryant's gaze and rolled his eyes. "No, sir."

"Well, when you do, that's when we'll talk about it." The President walked out of the office and headed back to the reception hall, leaving Chief of Staff Ramsey and General Mitchell to stare blankly at each other.

CHAPTER 37

Arts Center
Eastport, Maine
Friday, December 31st, 9:38 P.M.

What distinguishes man from the rest of animals
is his ability to do artificial things.

~ **KURT VONNEGUT,**
Player Piano

D inner was over by 9:30, just in time for the two couples to make the 9:45 production at the Arts Center. Tonight there would be two short plays, both comedies, focusing on, to quote the playbill, "The Funny Things that Can Happen when Modern Technology has a Mind of its Own." The four found seats near the front of the auditorium. Lee looked at the playbill and shook his head.

"What's wrong, Lee?" asked Liz.

"I just can't believe they're doing these two pieces of comedy tonight."

"Why not?"

"I don't know . . . I just find it strange that this is what they're doing."

Liz looked puzzled. Lee shrugged and said nothing more. He couldn't explain what he was thinking or feeling without getting into a much longer conversation that he really didn't want to have with her. The first was "The Not-So-Smart Smartphone" that apparently loved pizza and kept crank ordering it for everyone on its owner's Facebook friends list, repeatedly. The second, "The Tornado" about a weather center computer that apparently enjoyed scaring the bejesus out of people by issuing emergency weather alerts even when there was no emergency weather. In a variation on "The Boy who Cried Wolf," the human forecasters began to ignore these weather alerts and failed to warn the public of a tornado that almost destroyed the community.

True to the history of television sitcoms, the problem was addressed in an hour, even with two unplanned intermissions due to electrical problems in the theater.

When the last play ended at 10:45, they followed the crowd to Bank Square. The dropping of the Maple Leaf went off without a hitch. People sang *O Canada*, but as the crowd dispersed into the cafés and shops to wait for midnight, drumming and chanting erupted suddenly from the back.

The People of the Dawn were joining other native people to protest a Canadian government decision to ignore treaties with their Native citizens and allow major corporations to drill for natural gas and mine for precious metals on—or, more correctly, under—Native land. They carried signs: "Protect Native Rights." "Honor Treaties with your Native Citizens." But both Lee and Liz recognized the chanting and drumming from the afternoon ceremony. The Prayer of Forgiveness. The Humble Song. What else were they communicating in their dancing and chanting? And to whom? Most of the crowd watched. Some joined in as the Passamaquoddy circled the square chanting and drumming.

"Boy, you can understand why that sound sent fear through the hearts of the early white settlers," said Liz, and Lee nodded.

The protest stayed peaceful, although two Canadian Mounties in their bright red uniforms, imported for the Maple Leaf ceremony, chose to withdraw into the lobby of the museum. The CNN reporters covering the Sardine Drop didn't seem that interested in the protest. Native people being screwed yet again wasn't really new news. Besides, this was First Night, New Year's Eve. News needed to be good, not about conflict and protest.

After about twenty minutes, the crowd dispersed, some to have one last drink before midnight, others just to get warm. Lee and Liz took in some free entertainment on the second floor of the museum. A young man from the nearby town of Lubec—ten minutes by boat and an hour and fifteen minutes by car—sang about the people of the County who stood together in good and bad times and took care of their own. The crowd loved it.

Lee and Liz had lost track of Mike and June.

CHAPTER 38

White House
Washington, DC
Friday, December 31st, 11:10 P.M.

President Bryant was sitting on a couch in his private quarters, watching the FOX news affiliate, when Chief of Staff Ramsey knocked on the door and entered. The President looked up.

"Jim, give me some good news. It's a beautiful night. Clear, warm, a nice breeze." He hated the cold, wet, and dark days of early winter in DC.

"Okay, sir. Mitchell says the transmissions from Beta 17 have slowed and the number of sightings in the last hour or two has dropped to almost zero. And the Europeans seem to have calmed down and gone to bed."

"Well, then, stand down; drop the alert status. I'm looking forward to sitting right here with my beautiful wife and watching the ball drop in Times Square. I missed it last year."

"I remember, sir," said Ramsey.

"That crazy stuff going on in Egypt, I think. But we handled it."

"Actually, sir, it kind of handled itself."

The President nodded and continued to watch the broadcast. FOX gave little airtime to the UFO story. Instead, it focused on Senator Clayton and what they labeled as her "anti-tech movement," which the Heritage Foundation spokeswoman warned could "undermine our economy and hinder job development."

CHAPTER 39

Bank Square
Eastport, Maine
Friday, December 31st, 11:15 P.M.

The crowd in Bank Square was starting to gather again. The midnight hour was just a few minutes away. Mike and June were there already, talking to someone Lee didn't know. He assumed it might be the new fire chief. June looked bored, until she caught Liz's eye. They both smiled and dove into a passionate conversation about a new shop on Water Street that had just opened this season.

Lee wandered over and stood next to Mike waiting, a bit nervously, to be introduced. He had a sense that something was going to happen and soon. He hadn't slept well at all since his return. The same dream, again very vivid and lifelike, had come every night.

In the dream, he was in a crowd of people who were moving but making no sound. Their features and gestures were distorted and slowed, as was time and space. Lee tried to speak, to scream, but no words would come. He tried to move, run away, but his feet were frozen in place He felt like he was trapped in a Salvador Dali painting. He usually woke in a cold sweat.

"Dr. Brazil." He realized that Mike was talking to him. "I'd like for you to meet Chief Cutler."

Lee still felt distracted but extended his hand.

"Joe," the stranger responded and took Lee's hand. He had a firm grip and looked Lee in the eye as he talked. In his mid to late forties, he appeared sure of himself. The old chief, whom Lee had met before, had retired and, according to the new chief, was at home watching it all on Community Cable.

"So, Joe tells me that things are really hopping tonight," said Mike.

Joe agreed. "Oh, yeah. Lights in the sky. UFOs. But nobody wants to make a formal report. Paperwork, I guess." He chuckled. "Earlier tonight, I was listening to traffic at the Jetport. One of the—whatever you want to call them—nearly hit a United from Chicago. Homeland Security has increased the alert status."

"Well, I talked with Robert, our police chief in Winterpool, and he says everything down there is calm. But a few weeks ago . . ." Mike's voice faded.

Lee's face began to flush. It's starting, he thought—just breathe. What was starting, he didn't know.

"Well, I never saw anything like that before," said Mike, finishing his story about the UFO in Winterpool two weeks before.

"Hang on, Mike," Chief Cutler said, pulling his radio from his jacket. "Let me take this . . . Go ahead."

"Chief, have you been following what's happening in DC?" asked the excited dispatcher. "They scrambled jets from Andrews. Turn on 6, the 11 o'clock news . . . I've got it on." His voice continued to rise. "Mother of God, look at that. An array of lights—four, five, six of 'em. What the hell is that? Took off like a bat out of hell to the northeast. Coming our way."

"Who knows what's going on?" said Mike, shaking his head but smiling. "Maybe our friends from another world are finally going to pay the President a visit." Mike looked at Lee. All three men smiled nervously.

They pushed their way through the crowd, herding the two women— who were still talking about the shop on Water Street— toward a huge monitor that the town had set up in front of the museum. The NBC affiliate was just starting coverage of Times Square. It was 11:35.

"It's an amazing night here in New York," said the host. "The sky is clear and the crowd seems to be enjoying the weather and the entertainment. So, Karen, who are you talking with down there?"

The camera panned the crowd. People were waving and

screaming. Karen was attempting to interview a mildly inebriated couple from Indianapolis who had just gotten married.

Mike turned to Lee. "New York doesn't seem too concerned about the lights in the sky or the UFOs in DC."

Chief Cutler broke in. "And I don't think we should be either . . . It's 11:38, so on with our show." He turned off the audio on the monitor. The crowd outside the museum was growing, with people streaming out of Water Street bars and restaurants. The chief took his position on the podium and attempted a sound check, but his words were lost over the noise, which continued to increase as the clock ticked toward midnight.

Lee hadn't said anything for the last few minutes, even when Liz told him that Dru had texted that she and Rob weren't going to make it in time for the Sardine Drop and would watch on cable from their room.

Mike nudged Lee's arm. "Robert just texted me from home. The fighters in DC have returned to Andrews. Homeland Security has sounded an all clear."

Lee didn't speak.

Mike tried again. "Sounds like we're going to have a New Year's Eve with no more interruptions."

Lee still didn't respond.

"You okay, Lee?" asked Mike.

Lee nodded and sighed, realizing that he'd been holding his breath. He smiled and found Liz in the crowd.

"Are you okay, Lee? You look a little pale. What's up?"

"Oh, nothing. Nothing but—everything is okay, I think."

Liz looked concerned. "What do you mean, you think?"

Lee attempted a reassuring smile, but Liz wasn't buying it.

"Lee," she said sternly, elongating his name.

"Relax, relax, we're fine." Lee smiled again. I hope, he thought.

"I can't hear you," hollered Liz, as the two large speakers near the podium came alive and boomed out Chief Cutler's voice:

"Are you ready for 2028?" The crowd, responded by screaming a mixture of "Yes" and "Hell, yes," peppered with other obscenities.

The chief continued to work the crowd. "Are you ready for 2027 to be over?" This question drew a similar response.

"Okay. Are you folks ready up there?" The spotlight found two people hanging out of a third-story window at the museum, preparing to lower the eight-foot sardine. They waved. The crowd cheered.

"Are you ready for the Sardine Drop?" asked the Chief. The screaming horde went wild again.

Lee glanced at the digital clock set up in a museum window: 11:59:06.

The throng waited with anticipation as the remaining seconds of the old year ticked away. The sardine began its descent, as did the giant glass ball in Times Square. The crowd picked up the count at "Ten, nine . . .

No one else seemed to notice the sudden gust of warm air. Lee scanned the crowd, then his eyes returned to rest on Liz.

"Four, three, two, one."

The crystal ball in Times Square and the Sardine in Eastport were perfectly synchronized this year. They reached their mark just as the clock on the town hall struck midnight.

As the clock continued to strike, the sardine, the giant monitor, and the town of Eastport went dark. For a few moments, the only light was starlight. Orion and the winter constellations were rising in the moonless sky.

At first, everyone ignored the power outage; it had become a common occurrence. They continued shouting, "Happy New Year!" Couples embraced and kissed. People blew horns.

Then people waited. When it became evident that the lights weren't going to click back on immediately, lighters and matches began flicking.

Even a couple of candles appeared. People began searching for their cellphones, complaining when they wouldn't turn on.

Lee turned to kiss Liz, but just as their lips met, Chief Cutler and his assistant shoved them out of the way.

"Make way! Make way," he yelled. "Randy, give me that cord." They were trying to get the emergency generators started. As the crowd settled and began to accept their plight, a few started singing *Auld Lang Syne.* Others joined in.

The Chief finally got the emergency generators started, and a bank of lights popped on, as did the TV monitor. The crystal ball and Times Square were dark, except for an occasional flashlight and thousands of glow sticks.

"Well, folks," Brian, the host, was saying, "I'm not sure what's happening right now, but the authorities assure me that the power will be restored momentarily."

The CNN crew in Eastport scrambled to get their cameras back on but couldn't. People were telling stories about previous power outages. As they realized that the power was also out in New York City, they began to assemble in front of the television monitor. The NBC news cameras panned the buildings. Emergency lighting was coming on. Police and fire officials were setting up emergency light banks. The hum of generators competed with the Times Square crowd.

Brian continued, "It's an amazingly warm night in New York City, with a gentle breeze blowing out of the west. The sky is clear, and this may be the first time that the stars have been seen in Times Square since the power outages of the 1960s. People seem amazingly calm and are in good spirits. I guess we'll just have to wait for the utilities folks here in the city to do their job. I'm sure they will. I'm sure the power will be back . . ."

Mike and Chief Cutler were talking. Mike motioned for Lee to join them. Liz grabbed his hand. "I'm coming too." Lee squeezed her hand.

She'd never been comfortable in a crowd, especially in the dark. She motioned for June to follow, which she did.

"Well, folks," said Chief Cutler, "we've got a situation. The power's out everywhere."

"In the state?" asked Liz.

"Looks like it's out in the U.S. and in Canada."

"And other countries?" asked Lee.

"That's what they're saying," said Cutler. He gave Lee a strange look.

"You don't seem surprised by that, Dr. Brazil."

Lee was aware of the blood rushing to his face. He was sure that he looked guilty of something.

"Well, I . . . I don't know what to say. I'm as surprised as everyone."

"You . . ."

Mike cut Cutler off. "I know Brazil. He's okay, Chief."

"Well." Chief Cutler hesitated momentarily then went on with what he was saying. "The only place with power in this town is the aid station and the fire hall. It's the damnedest thing I've ever seen."

"I know," said Mike. "Even power companies can't explain it. Lights are out all the way down the coast, and no phones are working except emergency personnel's. The only number anyone else can dial is 9-1-1."

A young man with his girlfriend in tow pushed his way into the circle. "Chief, our battery's dead, and what the heck is going on with the phones?"

"Look, son," said the Chief, with considerable irritation, "I got more to worry about than your damned battery and phone. Ask Jim if he can help you. He's over there trying to jump-start a car."

Colorful hoods decorated the Square and adjoining parking areas, as people tried various methods to start their cars, but with no luck. Jim was having no success jump-starting a car from his fire truck. Other emergency vehicles had pulled into the Square and were making similar efforts to no avail. Lee watched a young woman try to recharge her phone off an electrical outlet from a fire truck. The phone didn't respond.

"Ours is dead, too," said another woman in tears. "And no one can get their car started."

At that moment, a gasp of disbelief emerged from those assembled in front of the big-screen television. The Chief's assistant pushed his way through the crowd, yelling for the Chief. "Chief, you've got to see this."

"Okay, okay. I'll be there in a second."

But his assistant insisted, "Right now, Chief." He started moving people aside, clearing the way for Cutler. Lee and Liz followed.

"Look Lee," said Liz.

"What the hell," the Chief echoed her tone of amazement.

The cameras in Times Square were focused on the Jumbotron, the only lighted sign in Times Square. But instead of carrying the usual ads for a cola or a camera, it was repeating the same short message over and over again.

DO JUSTICE. LOVE MERCY.
WALK HUMBLY WITH YOUR GOD.

People were muttering. "Some religious nut must be behind this whole thing," one man shouted.

"I told you, Margaret. It's the end times," said another.

"Who's running the show down there?" asked Cutler.

Liz turned to Lee, "What's going on?"

"I don't know, but I do know that that's from the Bible, perhaps even the Torah and the Koran."

"It's in Revelations," said another man in the crowd.

"No," Lee corrected. "The Book of Micah, I think. It's called 'The Great Requirement.'"

Another warm gust of wind blew from the west, tossing dried leaves and scraps of paper into the air. It seemed to have a calming effect on the crowd. Lee took a deep breath. He saw other people do the same.

People began making arrangements for where they might stay or what they might do. Emergency personnel gave up trying to start cars or power up cellphones and began ferrying people to their homes or the homes of friends. Some walked, very slowly Lee thought. In fact, everyone and everything seemed to had slowed, like in his dream. Only this time, he wasn't afraid. No one was. Some kind of acceptance seemed to have swept over the crowd. The chanting and drumming had stopped. The Square was relatively quiet. Only a few people milled around the edges, appearing uncertain of what to do next. In the distance over the hum of the generators, Lee could hear waves lapping at the shore. The tide was coming in.

CHAPTER 40

Side street near Bank Square
Eastport, Maine
Friday, December 31st, 11:28 P.M.

Lou and Jay had left the B&B late. Jay had decided to wash her hair at the last minute. Lou, as usual, was concerned about being on time. They'd had a hard time finding parking near the Square.

"I told you this would happen," he said. Jay didn't respond.

"What time is it?" asked Lou.

"Relax. We have time. It's just 1130."

"I see one." Loue squeezed his old SUV between two pickup trucks. "Okay, let's go," he snapped.

"Hang on, Lou. You know I can't walk as fast as you in these boots. The world won't end if we miss the Drop."

"How do you know? As crazy as things have been in the last few days."

They began walking toward Bank Square. "You know, I was remembering what our pal Thomas said that last day we were there."

Jay looked around to make sure no one was in earshot, but they were alone on the street. "You mean the part about getting the world's attention?"

"Yeah. Like firing a warning shot: 'Pay attention. Understand that you're not alone in the universe. Others care about the neighborhood.'"

"I don't know. I haven't thought about it much since we came back. That was years ago, so I guess I sort of blocked it out."

They could hear the crowd in the Square. People were still streaming out of bars and restaurants. They climbed over a snowbank and found a place in the crowd.

"We made it," said Lou.

"Told you we would," Jay responded.

The countdown was starting. On a giant television, the ball in Times Square slowly descended. Those lowering the sardine were trying to coordinate its descent with the ball's.

"I'm glad you suggested this, Jay" said Lou, "it's made the holidays easier for me this year."

"Good! I'm glad, Lou." She paused a few seconds "At least you got to see your grandkids this year. I think your daughters are finally accepting the divorce."

"Yeah." Lou brightened. "Maybe next year, we could bring them up here to see the sardine drop."

"That would be fine with me. I like them. Your daughters have raised them well."

He turned and looked at her. "You'd be fine with that?" He wanted to make sure of what he'd heard.

She smiled again and nodded.

"Five, four, three, two, one: Happy New Year" the crowd roared. The clock in the town hall struck midnight. Lou grabbed Jay and kissed her with real passion. Neither realized that the lights in the square and all the buildings around it were out until they heard a collective gasp and opened their eyes. For a moment, they were like everyone else, silent.

"I'll get out my trusty cell phone," said Lou, but the light didn't work. Neither did the phone. They looked around and saw other people doing the same thing with the same result.

"What's going on Lou?" asked Jay, her voice rising.

"I told you that I had a feeling something was going to happen. It's got to be Thomas and his clan. They're certainly capable of doing this."

"Maybe we should finally tell someone what we know. Maybe they'd believe us with all of this happening," Jay suggested.

"I doubt it. They'll just think we're crazy."

"Look! There's the police chief." Jay pushed through the crowd, not waiting for Lou, who trailed behind.

"Chief Cutler! Chief Cutler!" Jay shouted. "We have to tell you something."

"What?" asked Cutler. "That your car won't start, and your phone doesn't work?"

"No, no!" Jay tried to catch her breath. "We think we know who caused the power outage tonight."

"Now that I would be interested in hearing. Step over here." He led Jay into a tent set up on the edge of the crowd. Lou followed.

"Now little lady, tell me what you know."

"Well," she turned to Lou, who nodded.

"Lou and I were . . . Well, I guess you would say abducted."

"By terrorists?" asked the chief, leaning toward her.

"Well, No." She turned to Lou again.

"This was a few years ago," he offered.

"What's that got to do with what's happening tonight?" The chief looked directly at Lou.

"I'm not sure you will believe us, but . . ."

"I may not, but go on. I don't have all night. As you can see, I'm a little busy."

"Okay." Lou took a deep breath and blurted, "There's an alien civilization living under the Sea near Bermuda."

"Oh Christ. You're right, I don't believe you. Jim!" Cutler called for one of his officers

Jay tried her luck. "You need to listen to us. They're sending a message. We need to realize we aren't alone in this universe."

"Jim get these two wackos out of here. I don't have time to deal with their craziness."

Cutler looked at Lou again. "Trying to make a joke out of this could get you arrested."

"We're not crazy!" shouted Jay. It's no joke! We saw them with our own eyes."

216

"Come on folks, we don't have time for this," said Jim, taking Lou by the arm. Jay followed. Cutler just shook his head and muttered something.

When they were a few feet from the tent, Jay said, "Well, we tried."

"That we did," Lou agreed. "But I told you this would happen if we ever told anyone. And maybe it's better that way. As crazy as President Bryant is, he might try to find and destroy Thomas and the others. We shouldn't say any more about this. Let the chief write us off as two crazies making a bad joke."

"I think that tonight is just the beginning. Maybe they'll do more. Maybe they *will* get the world's attention," said Jay.

"You know, we sort of helped tonight to happen by what we did for Thomas and his people. I think we should just sit back and see what happens next."

She nodded and pulled her hat down over her ears. "I'm cold. The woodstove at the B and B would feel really good. I assume *it* still works." They both laughed.

"Well, it's a bit of a hike back there. I guess we need to get started." Jay groaned.

As they began to walk in the direction of Winton House, it started to snow again.

CHAPTER 41

Shot's Bar
Hamilton, Bermuda
Saturday, January 1, 2028, 12:05 A.M.

People are crazy. Times are strange. I'm locked in tight.
I'm out of range. I used to care, but things have changed.

~ Bob Dylan,

Things Have Changed

Jeff had been at the bar since late afternoon. He wasn't sure of the day but guessed that it must be the first of January, 2028. The noisy crowd had spent most of the last half hour wishing each other a Happy New Year. He doubted that this year would be any better than the last. TransSea's "up front" money was already gone: The mortgage. Doctor bills for the kids.

He'd spent most of the last week tied to a chair somewhere in Bermuda. His captors, Hollocore Security, hadn't fed him the first day and then only stale sandwiches on the second and third days. They seemed unsure what to do with him but after five days decided that a good beating would be sufficient. He didn't remember much about the beating. He just remembered waking up in a ditch near the airport yesterday morning.

He'd used someone's phone to call Judy collect, and she'd wired him enough money for a room for the night. She'd been worried sick but hadn't known what to do but wait and pray. She'd also sent enough money for food and a ticket home, but all flights out were booked until New Year's Day.

Jeff's ribs ached, as did his head, although some of the swelling had gone down. He missed Judy and the kids. He missed them so much. Unfortunately, he'd used most of the money she'd wired here at the bar.

Jeff focused on the television hanging over the bar. He wanted to see the ball drop in Times Square. He remembered when he and his wife had been there. Years ago, before the children. He couldn't hear what was going on, but he watched the ball's slow descent. He counted with it: four, three, two, one. Nothing. The lights in the bar flickered and went off. But for some reason, the television stayed on. The ball was dark. The power was out in New York, too. He wondered what was happening. Were Judy and the kids okay? He was sure she'd be up; they always watched the ball drop.

Jeff decided that, like with everything else, he could do little about it. He ordered another beer and tried not to think about the past week. Or what he'd do next. A few people in the bar complained about their cell phones not working, but most people seemed to not care that the power was out.

CHAPTER 42

St. Paul's Church Courtyard
St. Georges, Bermuda
Saturday, January 1st, 12:51 A.M. Atlantic Time

Father Allen had just concluded midnight mass and walked out into the courtyard to visit with his old friend David before returning to his quarters.

"So, what did you think of my message?"

"The Great Requirement—kindness, justice, humility— that's a tall order for humanity. I don't know."

"You sound very skeptical, David. As I was preparing the message, I noticed that I wasn't alone. This theme is being conveyed to congregations across the world tonight."

"But, Father, do you think that people will change without being forced?"

"I don't know. We certainly seem to be creating smarter machines." The priest sighed. "But I would agree; unfortunately, we seem to be no better at mastering anger, greed, or jealousy than we've ever been." Father Allen paused and stared out at the lights of St. Georges. "But I have a feeling that something will happen tonight to change that."

"You're not alone. I feel it, too. There have been more sightings of the lights tonight than I can ever remember. Something is happening."

"And I believe that, in some way, we and our visitors last week are playing a role in what is about to happen."

"You're certainly more of a believer and optimist than I am, Father."

"Maybe so, David. Maybe so. I guess we'll see."

It was a clear night, with a gentle, warm wind blowing through the tall pines in the courtyard. They could see the lights of Hamilton in the distance.

Father Allen looked at his watch. "Well, in a few seconds it will be the New Year in New York. I hope that it will be a good one."

"I . . ." As David started to speak, the lights of the island started going off. First Hamilton, then St. Georges, then the rest, but neither David nor Father Allen seemed alarmed.

"It's starting, isn't it, Father?"

"Yes, David, I believe it is."

Exactly what was starting they didn't know.

Condominium of Joann Lawrence
Portland, Maine
Same Day, 12:07 A.M. EST

When the power went off, Joann waited for the emergency lighting in her condo to pop on. And it did. She picked up the large flashlight that she had by her chair for just such an emergency and prided herself on being prepared. She tried to turn it on but couldn't. I must have forgotten to change the batteries, she thought. I'll put that on my list.

She decided not to wait for the lights to come back on. They always did within an hour, but she was tired. She checked the doors and windows and trudged upstairs. She turned the heat down for when the power came back on but threw a couple of extra blankets on the bed in case it didn't. Being a Mainer, she opened a window in her bedroom and was surprised that it had gotten warmer rather than colder outside. That's odd, she thought, as she tucked herself in. She drifted off to sleep, imagining the sound and feel of a warm, gentle breeze blowing through the large palm that stood outside her bedroom window in Florida.

CHAPTER 43

The White House
Washington, DC
Saturday, January 1st, 1:07 A.M.

There must be virtue in imperfection for man is
imperfect and man is a creation of God.

~ KURT VONNEGUT,
Player Piano

T he President sat at a desk in the Situation Room with General Mitchell, the Secretary of Defense, and the Secretary of State. He appeared dazed and befuddled by the events of the last hour.

General Mitchell spoke. "The power outages are selective, sir. The military, public safety, and healthcare are operating as usual. But the general public and corporations have no power." Jeff O'Donnell, the Secretary of Transportation, arrived and took his seat in the circle forming around the President, who acknowledged him. "So, Jeff, what good news do you bring me?"

He was out of breath. "I don't know, sir. I guess the good news is that all commercial and civil flights are landing without problems, but we've ordered them all down anyway. Only medical and military flights can take off. Trains and subway cars arrive at their stations but lose power as soon as they do. Ships at sea are reporting no problems, but once they make port, they lose power and the ability to unload their cargo." O'Donnell looked down at his hands. "Sir, I have no explanation for any of this. As I heard General Mitchell saying as I entered the room, this is selective. But how and why . . . I don't know."

President Bryant looked at his Secretary of Defense, who acknowledged in a perplexed and almost apologetic tone that the armed forces were experiencing no problems. The Secretary of Health and Human Services concurred, adding that she'd had no reported fatalities or injuries related to the communication and power outages.

The President shook his head and raised his voice. "How is that possible? That's ridiculous. Maybe they just haven't been reported. This must be a cyberattack of some kind. The Iranians . . . the Chinese must be up to something . . . the North Koreans? Yes, it must be that little SOB."

"No, Mr. President," corrected the Secretary of Defense. "Our sources say that it's not a cyberattack. Our enemies aren't capable of doing this."

"So, what does the weather service say?"

"Well, in the last few hours, the entire Earth's atmosphere has warmed significantly. We've never recorded this before and really have no idea what's causing it. Such sudden change could be related to global warming." The president cut him off. He and his base didn't believe in global warming. He turned to the Secretary of Homeland Security, Jeff Fram, who was on his Q-pad. He looked up. "Well, Mr. President, I'm not sure what I should report. 9-1-1 and emergency numbers are all operating. The lines were initially swamped with calls, but now the frequency seems to have decreased. Our folks are in position and ready to respond and coordinate our efforts with local police departments and fire and rescue services, but we haven't had to. The mass hysteria that we expected from such an event hasn't occurred. I can't explain why, except to say that a good percentage of the country went to bed before the event occurred . . . and most people appear to be assuming that the lights will come back on. Plus, the weather is amazingly warm for this time of year. And another factor I should mention is that the electromagnetic field surrounding our planet seems to have been suddenly significantly reduced by this power outage."

The president was rolling his eyes, so the Secretary stopped. "I guess all I have to report is good news."

"Well, as you say, perhaps they haven't realized what's happening. Well . . . well, I can't believe all this . . . is possible," said the President. "And what about that Bible verse plastered across the Jumbotron in Times Square?"

The Secretary of State responded, "Similar verses from the Koran and other religious texts have appeared on electronic bulletin boards and signs across the world."

"Well," said the president, "shut the damn thing down! At least the one in Times Square!" The president stood up and ran his right hand through his dyed, reddish-blond hair. "I mean, I think it's a great Bible verse. I memorized it in Sunday school. But the left-wingers like Clayton will . . . well, I don't know what they'll do. But do something about it."

Chief of Staff Ramsey grimaced. "We've tried, sir, to turn it off. But it seems to be controlled by . . . well, we don't know what or who is controlling it."

General Mitchell started to speak, but President Bryant cut him off. "Don't start with me again about aliens."

Ramsey broke in. "Sir, we have to assume that these events are not random, that some force . . . some form of intelligence, is orchestrating it."

"Well . . . well . . ." The President, who had sat down again pulled himself out of his chair and faced his Cabinet. He took a deep breath. "I'm not ready to accept that . . . not yet. I want to stand for reelection, and if I tell the American people that aliens are shutting off their lights and their Q-Pads and are trying to hold a tent revival in Times Square . . . well?" He looked at his Chief of Staff. "Jim, I need to talk with you. Thank you, gentlemen. Please excuse us."

Jim and the President moved quickly to a private office. President Bryant, who remained standing, began to pace.

"Jim, I'm thinking."

"I can see that, sir."

"I..." He stopped.

Jim waited a few moments then said, "Sir, the media is demanding a statement from you. You need to tell the American people something very soon. Now, here's what I've done . . ."

Bryant hated the media, and the feeling was mutual, so he'd finally taken Jim's advice and let him deal with them. He still tweeted, but less.

The President showed some relief and sat down to listen to the man who had pulled him through several difficult times in the past.

"Mr. President, two hours ago, I took the liberty of asking the Federal Emergency Management Agency to begin setting up viewing and listening areas across the country."

"Good, good," said Bryant. "They've been wanting to use their new toys. Here's a perfect opportunity."

Jim smiled and nodded. The President was referring to large generator- powered projection screens and amplifiers through which the Emergency Broadcasting System could reach citizens in the event of a massive power failure. Hollocore had received the government contract to create the system—an expensive piece of technology that had never been tested in a real emergency.

"They can't accuse me of being like Trump, slow to respond with the first hurricane that hit Puerto Rico," said the President. "When a second one hit that godforsaken place, I sent in federal troops."Again, Jim nodded and smiled. "Mr. President, here's what I would suggest you say to the American people."

CHAPTER 44

Hollocore Global Operations Center
Undisclosed Location
Dallas, Texas
Saturday, January 1st, 1:33 A.M.

So it goes . . .
~ Kurt Vonnegut

When Dick Chambers burst through the door of the Operations Center, activity and conversation ceased and everyone focused on him. "Where the hell is Reggie Brown?"

Brown popped up from his chair. "Here, sir."

"In my office, now!"

Chambers, head down like a charging bull, started for his office, just off the main control room. Brown quickly followed.

Chambers slammed the door. "What's going on? You told me two months ago that you and your staff had determined that the problems in data transmission were the result of solar activity. I believed you."

Brown was speechless.

"So, what's going on tonight? The President tells me *his* people believe that the source of both that problem and the global power failure we're experiencing tonight is a giant rock."

"An asteroid," Brown choked out.

"An asteroid that you told me was just a giant rock."

"Yes, I did, sir. But in the last twenty-four hours it appears to be the source of a variety of transmissions."

Chambers mumbled something about the SOB's at TransSea then demanded, "Where the hell is Dr. Carter? I want to Carter right now."

"I'll get him, sir." Brown picked up the intercom. "Connie, tell Dr. Carter to join us . . . immediately."

Within seconds, Carter was in the room, and Chambers turned to him. "This rock causing all the problems has a name, doesn't it, Carter?"

"Yes, sir. 1992 Beta-17."

"This is the asteroid," his voice rose, "that TransSea has sent a number of probes to in the last two years."

"Yes, sir. It will pass very close to Earth in the next few days. As you know, TransSea has launched a robotic mining unit that will land on Beta- 17 and take core samples."

"You advised us not to proceed with our plans for such a mission."

"Yes, sir." Carter was beginning to perspire.

"You advised myself and the Board that such a mission as TransSea is now executing would be too risky. You said, 'a fool's errand,' as I recall." He waited. "You said that we should focus on getting the contract to develop the supercomputer."

Carter nodded but didn't speak. He looked down at the floor.

"So how do you feel about that decision tonight, Dr. Carter?"

"I don't know, sir."

"Well, I do," said Chambers. "It would appear that TransSea was right. That giant rock *is* worth exploring. The electronic transmissions that Beta- 17 is emitting tonight are off the chart!"

Carter looked up. His face was reddening by the minute. "Yes, I know, sir. How and from what source this energy is derived, we don't know."

"And we *won't* know, because we chose not to go there. TransSea is there and we aren't, right, Dr. Carter? And what we *do* know is that those who control the sources of energy control our world." Chambers was now pacing around the room, glaring at Brown then Carter in turn.

"Do you two realize how much money we're losing every hour our network is down? This could bankrupt the company!"

Carter nodded and Brown responded, "Yes, I know, sir." "Well, then, what are we doing about this mess?" Neither man replied.

Suddenly, Chambers seemed unsteady on his feet and nearly fell into his chair. Carter and Brown waited. Finally, Carter asked, "Sir, are you okay?"

Chambers didn't respond right away. After some seconds, he said, "I don't know," certainly an usual response for him. "Please," another unusual response . . . "Please open that window and turn off that damn filtration unit. I could use some fresh air."

The two complied and waited.

"I feel warm . . . all over," said Chambers.

"Sir, I think we should call medical," Carter advised. "No, no," objected Chambers. "It actually feels . . . good." He smiled.

Carter and Brown looked puzzled. Neither had ever seen him smile.

"I'm okay, I think," he said. "Gentlemen, go home to your families."

The men hesitated. They'd never heard Chambers acknowledge that employees had families, much less suggest that they should leave work to be with them.

"Go! Go!" he said again. And they complied.

CHAPTER 45

Eastport, Maine
Saturday, January 1st, 1:17 A.M.

Faith is the substance of things hoped for,
the evidence of things not seen.

~ Hebrews

The next hour passed quickly. People continued to exchange stories and ask each other what was happening. NBC was reporting power failures, not just in Eastport and New York City, but across the globe. People were expressing disbelief, and a strange thing was happening. People were focusing on the same screen, hearing the same news coverage, and starting to talk to each other—face to face. And no one panicked.

People would leave and then return to the Square to ask the chief for help, but his small department was overwhelmed.

"Lee, honey," whispered Liz, "my feet are awfully cold."

"We can go back to Jane's." Lee wasn't sure that he could assist Mike and the chief any further. In fact, they could do little other than help people find places for the night. "We'll have to walk."

"I think we should try the car. You just replaced the battery."

"Liz, honey, trust me," Lee said with visible irritation. "It won't work." She started to object but stopped herself. Like most of the people in the Square that night, she didn't seem as upset as Lee thought she would be.

He'd spent most of the last hour helping Mike and just observing the scene. Chief Cutler had said that people were taking all this much better than he expected. Some people who he thought would raise a ruckus and threaten to sue his department and the power company hadn't. Lee had watched a young man whom the Chief said was a troublemaker try to recharge his cellphone in the Chief's truck without success. Instead of complaining, he'd thanked the Chief and asked if he could do anything to assist. Most people seemed to accept their inability to alter the situation. Indeed, some of the hurry sickness that afflicts society had abated, at least for a few hours. The I-gotta-have-it-now syndrome had weakened.

As they started to leave Bank Square, Lee saw Mike standing with Chief Cutler and the Eastport Police Chief, Roger Dutro. "Come on, Liz, let's talk with them before we leave."

They made their way through the crowd, which appeared to be growing. And the chanting and drumming had begun again. As they approached the trio, Cutler, who'd served in military intelligence for many years, was saying something about the reasons why the military system might still be functioning.

Mike objected, "Joe, I think they could have knocked out the military systems if they, or it, wanted to, but that hasn't happened, at least not yet. We know that hospitals and public safety units have power, as do the major television networks. EMS vehicles are running. 9-1-1 is working, but everything else isn't. It's very selective, Joe. Whoever or whatever is behind this must know that if they took away our weapons systems or guns, they would create total panic."

"Well, maybe you're right, Mike," Cutler said begrudgingly.

Mike turned to Lee and Liz, who'd been standing silently, listening. "What do the two of you think? You've got the doctorate."

"I agree with you, Mike; it is selective," said Lee. "And I don't think that nature or the sun is the cause. Some form of intelligence is controlling what's happening."

"That's ridiculous," Cutler scoffed.

Mike came to Lee's defense. "Well, I don't know about that, Joe. Can you explain it any other way?" Cutler was silent. "I just know that I need to keep in touch with Chief Moore and, if need be, drive back to Winterpool tonight. Excuse me."

Cutler again eyed Lee with suspicion while he and Liz waited for Mike to be off the radio. The call was short; Chief Moore had nothing to report. In most ways, it was a typical New Year's Eve in Winterpool. Quiet.

"Well, Mike, I think Liz and I are going to go back to Winton House.Mike started to walk with them. "Lee, you're the psychologist. Tell me why we aren't seeing the mass panic that everyone predicted would occur if something like this happened. Why aren't people more upset? Why are things so damn calm? It gives me a chill."

They walked past the big-screen television. "Look at those folks in Times Square, Lee. Most of them are just standing there. They seem to be waiting for something. And look around us: the dancing and drumming— they seem to be enjoying themselves . . . and this weird weather." He shook his head. "You even look more relaxed now than you did earlier."

Lee wasn't exactly sure why, but he did feel more relaxed. He guessed it was because something was actually happening; he didn't have to anticipate or wait for it.

"Well, Mike, I guess I could give you the usual explanation: People may still be in a state of shock."

"And a lot of folks aren't even aware of the situation. And what's happening isn't what people might expect," said Liz.

"That's right, Mike. No one has seen flying saucers, death rays, screaming people, or exploding buildings. We've had no violence or hysteria." Lee paused. "I don't know, but those two impulses are wired into our DNA. Why they haven't emerged yet, I can't say. But if power isn't restored in a few hours, I don't know what will happen." Lee grimaced and shrugged. "I assume that we may revert back to our old selves."

They walked on. "Well, I hope not," said Mike. "I've been thinking of an article I read recently about how repeated exposure to microwaves affects the human brain. I know that you know what I'm talking about."

Lee nodded. He remembered the article in *Science*.

"Maybe our electrical systems have been affected by all of this tonight, just like the power grid. Maybe something has changed in us. Maybe we've been powered down."

"You may be right," Lee agreed. "You know, this may sound crazy, but I've had some strange dreams in the last few weeks about something like this happening. I was . . ."

Mike's radio went off. Just as well, thought Lee. He wasn't sure that he was ready to talk to Mike about the dreams. People, even Mike, always expected folks in Lee's profession to be just a little strange themselves.

"Well, I guess I need to stay and help Cutler and Dutro."

"June is welcome to walk back to the B&B with us," said Liz.

"Thanks, but I think she'll want to stay with me, given the situation."

They looked back at the giant television. Apparently, the news services hadn't found anyone to blame yet. Villains were in short supply, which was very strange and quite frustrating for those who needed a scapegoat.

Lee and Liz continued their walk back to the B&B. They found the old Subaru in the dark, and Lee dug out a hand-crank radio and flashlight. They walked on slowly and carefully, listening to the whine of emergency generators across the town. In those homes, lights were on; in others, oil lanterns flickered. Most were dark; their residents had apparently given up and gone to bed, assuming that the power would be back on by morning.

Lee thought about the message of justice, mercy, and humility. He'd learned that bit of scripture as a child from his grandfather, who had lived his life by those words. Lee remembered his Uncle Tommy and twin aunts Jean and Jane talking about how his grandfather, an attorney and businessman, managed his businesses during the first

Great Depression. He'd owned a number of houses that he rented out to tenants who, during the Depression, were unable to pay rent, but he let them stay. He'd also owned a general store at that time and allowed customers to charge groceries when they had no money, which was often the case. Most were never able to pay their bills. His grandfather went bankrupt during the Depression. He lost his store, and his home was later sold for taxes. The Depression destroyed him financially, like it had so many others, but his acts of kindness and his sense of what was just created a level of respect and gratitude in his community that outlived him.

Liz interrupted his musing. "Lee, you seem to know something about all of this."

"Maybe someone's trying to tell us something."

"What are you talking about?" asked Liz, with irritation tinged by desperation. "You know something about this that you're not telling me?"

Lee looked away.

"Tell me!" She grabbed Lee's arm.

"Liz, look," he said with more force than he intended, "a lot of weird things happened to me while I was away." He sounded apologetic.

"What do you mean? Does this have anything to do with those strange dreams you've been having?"

He wasn't sure what to say. "The problem is I don't know how much was and is real and how much I imagined or dreamed."

"The dreams told you this was going to happen, didn't they?"

"No, no." He insisted at first. "Well, not exactly," he finally said.

"Oh." She stopped and faced him, but he spoke before she could.

"I just don't know how to explain it to you. If I say more now, before figuring it out myself, you'll only have more questions that I can't answer."

They climbed the steps to the porch of Winton House in silence. At the top, Lee put his arms around her.

"Honey, I hope . . . things will be . . . okay. We're home, anyway."

Jane Giroux met them at the door with questions. "So tell me, what's the news from town?" She smiled nervously.

"EMS is working, so we're all safe," said Lee. "But no one's vehicle will run unless you work for public safety or the hospital, and no one's cell phone will work except to call 9-1-1. Land lines are out, too." Lee paused and smiled. "Other than that, everything is A-okay!" He chuckled.

"Lee," Liz scolded him.

"People may be scared and confused, but they're talking to each other about what's happening," said Liz, trying to sound positive.

"And the government has yet to find anyone to blame," Lee added with a smirk.

"Well, come get warm. I made some hot chocolate and a little hot toddy for those who indulge," she looked at Lee, "which is most of the group tonight. I think we could all probably use a drink on a night like this. Where are Mike and June and your daughter?"

"Dru and Rob are staying at the Williams B&B," said Liz.

"Mike and June are going to stay with Chief Cutler for a while," replied Lee, pulling off his coat and starting to help Liz with hers. "Not much to do except give people rides home."

Jane agreed. "Luckily, most people are staying in town. Joe sent a few over here. We'll put them up in the living room for the night. Oh, and the President is going to speak around two o'clock," Jane reported, clearly unsure as to whether this was a good thing or not.

"This New Year is certainly coming in with a bang." Liz made a weak effort at humor.

"Or a whimper," added Lee under his breath.

With considerable difficulty, Lee chose the hot chocolate. He and Liz took their drinks over to the wood stove. Other guests were scattered around the living room. One couple was talking. One sat silently. Most seemed lost.

Jane gave each couple an oil lamp that spilled a soft yellow glow onto the walls and furniture. Perhaps that was it, or maybe it was the hot chocolate or being away from the crowd, but Lee began to relax and feel more confident. He thought that he could put some of the pieces together.

Jane rushed into the room. "Bill got the generator going, so the TV is on, and the President is about to speak."

Lee and Liz and two other couples followed her into the library, just as he was introduced.

"Ladies and gentlemen . . . The President of the United States." Bryant was seated behind a desk in the Situation Room. He looked composed and presidential.

"My fellow Americans, in the last few hours, the people of the world have experienced an unprecedented electrical power failure. At this time, we do not know its source or how long it may last. But, believe me, I can assure you that no effort will be spared in rectifying this situation."

Lee turned to Liz. "Oh, God."

She tried to shush him, but he continued. "Bryant is best at creating crises, not fixing them. He'll probably use this one as justification for an attack on North Korea or Iran. I'm sure he believes that they're somehow behind all of this."

The President was saying, "The Good Lord has provided us with mild weather. Again, I stress that we are in no immediate danger. I urge calm. I've not yet determined the source of the problem, but I can assure you that I will . . ."

"He's going to find the source of the problem?" echoed Lee. "This guy couldn't find his ass with both hands and a map. But he is right about the weather. It's January, and the weather is so mild. How can that be?"

"Lee, please!"

He did fall silent but not because he was listening to Bryant. His was an inner dialogue.

"Liz, I think I understand something I didn't before."

"Just wait until he's finished," she hissed.

"I'm going upstairs." He leaned over and whispered to her, "It's about the alien."

CHAPTER 46

Condominium of Senator Nancy Clayton
Saturday, January 1st, 1:49 A.M.

Senator Clayton had no sooner fallen asleep than Fred Bolin was rapping on her bedroom door. "Senator!" he shouted but stopped himself and attempted to lower his voice and focus on trying to not sound as frightened as he was.

"You have to get up. They're here!"

Nancy Clayton pushed her graying blond hair out of her eyes and sat up in bed. "Who's here, Fred?" She grabbed for her robe, finally finding it at the foot of the bed, and started toward the door.

"The Capitol Police. They're here to take you to a safe location. They're evacuating the senators and representatives who are in DC."

Wanting to get an early start on the new year, she'd flown back to DC the day after Christmas. She'd celebrated Christmas with her daughter and her daughter's family and had spent some time with her granddaughter.

The visit had gone fine—better than in the first years after the divorce—but she still had little interest in holidays. In the last few years, she'd found herself spending more time in Washington and, consequently, more time working.

When the lights had gone out at midnight, she'd assumed that it was just another power outage that would be fixed by morning. She'd gone to bed and left orders not to be disturbed. Fred, who overreact to most things, said he would sleep in the guest room and wake her if necessary.

He hadn't disturbed her when the President made his address to the nation, although Fred now thought he should have. Something was certainly happening. But she was so tired. He worried about her.

"Fred, what is going on?" "I don't know, Senator. All I know is that the President has ordered an evacuation, and they say we need to leave immediately."

She walked back into her bedroom and looked out the window. Two black SUVs were parked in front of her condo with their emergency flashers on. Senator Clayton groaned, "What has that moron gotten us into now?" and headed for her bathroom.

CHAPTER 47

Winton House
Eastport, Maine
Saturday, January 1st, 1:50 A.M.

And God will delight when we are creators of justice.

~ Methodist Hymn

L iz followed Lee, as they found their way up the stairs, with the help of Jane's oil lamp. The room was warm; they'd banked the fire in the woodstove before going downtown.

Lee took a seat in one of the chairs by the window looking out on the bay and the Square. Liz opened the window. The air outside was amazingly warm. Lee offered her the more comfortable chair, and she sat down and immediately faced him.

"Now will you tell me what's going on?" she demanded. "Aliens? Really!"

"Yes. I think that the human race may have finally met our match. Some force in our universe is at work tonight. We've tried their patience, and they're saying to us, 'Time out.'"

"Oh, Lee, are you going to go off on that again? I think you've been watching too many *X File* reruns."

"Liz, I'm very serious about this. Don't try to deny what's happening," he snapped. "I don't know any other way to explain this. As I said walking over here, I haven't told you very much about what happened in Bermuda, because I didn't know how much I had imagined and how much was real."

"You were in Bermuda?"

"Yes, Liz, I was in Bermuda. What happened tonight isn't random.

239

And it's not being caused by solar flares or electromagnetic storms. You heard what Mike said. They could have shut everything down if they'd wanted to, but they didn't."

"But who are they? The Russians?"

He started to answer but didn't. If she really believed that the Russians could be at fault after what he'd already told her, she would continue to dismiss his real answer as "science fiction." So, he just continued his train of thought.

"Maybe they're demonstrating to us what practicing justice, kindness, and humility looks like. No death rays or exploding buildings or demands for surrender. In fact, I think that's the point," he said, his voice rising. "Yes, they could have destroyed us tonight or set us up to destroy ourselves, but they didn't." He looked out again at the square. "I don't think this will last very long. I don't see how it can." He shook his head. "There will be riots in the streets. Our economy and our whole social system will collapse if the world's power grids stay down." He stopped.

"They could've started that process tonight but chose not to," said Liz.

They continued to watch the crowd in Bank Square. The drumming was getting louder, and more people were joining the dancers.

"What happened to the package that we picked up in London? You delivered it to someone in Paris, didn't you?"

"No. I ended up having to carry it to Bermuda. I finally delivered a package to Jennings in Boston."

"Did you ever figure out what was in it?"

"It had something to do with this ultra-intelligent machine that we're building. Whoever is behind what's happening tonight doesn't want that computer built."

"When you say that you delivered 'a package' to Boston, was it the package we picked up?"

"I'm not sure. In the process of getting to Boston, I believe that the packages were switched. The one I delivered may be infected with viruses that will only frustrate those trying to build the computer." Lee shook his head again. "I'm really not completely sure what happened. I was drugged on the ship, and, since then, it's been difficult to figure out what really happened and what was a drug-induced dream."

"You were what! On what ship?"

"Honey, I've got a lot more to tell you. I'm sorry, but I didn't realize until a few minutes ago that all of this is real. I didn't imagine what happened in Bermuda; it was real! But that's not what's important right now."

"So, what is important right now?" asked Liz.

He could hear the frustration in her voice decreasing and sighed with relief. She was finally beginning to understand why he'd been only partially answering her questions.

"I think what is important now is what will happen today. The first day of the New Year."

"And what do you think will happen?"

"Maybe people will decide that the universe doesn't revolve around them." He looked at Liz. "Maybe we'll decide that justice, kindness, and humility are important to our survival and not just something nice to do when making money doesn't get in the way." Lee paused. "But I still don't understand exactly who or what is behind this."

"Well, I don't know, either, but they sure know how to make an entrance," said Liz.

They both laughed. The release and distraction felt good.

"I think they've taken their cue from *The Day the Earth Stood Still*."

"Maybe they'll look like Michael Rennie," said Lee.

"Or Keanu Reeves. I like the remake better."

"Well, I learned in Bermuda that they're definitely tired of being ignored and discounted and made only the stuff of science fiction."

They sat for a while, quietly drinking in the warm night air.

They focused on the present, not the past or future. They put away the hurry sickness, the 'I-want-it-all' syndrome. They were grateful for what they had and for the hope they felt about what might be. Maybe something had changed within them. And with the world. The change might only be temporary. But it felt good on this first day of the New Year.

"What time is it, Lee?"

"Close to three. We've got a few more hours before dawn. I think we should join the People of the Dawn in the Square and give a proper welcome to the first day of our New Year. Like the travel brochure says, 'Morning in America begins in Eastport, Maine.' Agreed?

Liz nodded.

"But first, let's try to get some sleep."

"I thought you'd never ask."

The two dressed for bed. Liz crawled in first. "I'm tired, and my feet are really cold."

"Your feet are always cold. I'm coming." Lee climbed in and pulled the cover up. "I think we're going to find out tomorrow our capacity as a human race to continue to deny reality."

"Did you say something?" Liz asked as she put her feet under his legs. "Oh, no-o-o-o," he said. "Jesum Crow, your feet are cold!"

"Remember that cabin we stayed in at Loon Lake?" asked Liz. "This reminds me of that. No power, just an oil lamp and a woodstove." She yawned and stretched. "Well, if you want to make people humble, just take away our electronics."

"It wasn't so bad at the lake, was it?" he asked.

"No. I really liked it," agreed Liz.

He put his arm around her, and they snuggled closer.

"Well, maybe we'll have to get used to life without our gadgets," he said. "I think that's going to be a very hard one for most of us."

"I'm sure you're right about that."

Lee and Liz finally drifted off to sleep. It took a while. They, like the rest of the world that night, weren't sure what was happening. But they tried to have faith that the force apparently now in control was benevolent, that tonight's situation was for good, not evil. Maybe we would grow up without destroying ourselves and the rest of the universe. Perhaps the first night of darkness would usher in a new age of light.

Lee was sure that the sun would rise again and that the power outage would end soon. But, for him, the most important unanswered question was who or what might people encounter on the first day of the New Year and, to quote Matthew and Mark, would we finally "Love our neighbors as ourselves"?

Outside, the early winter sky was moonless, clear, and bright with stars. Orion and the winter constellations were now high. The evening star, planet Mars, was rising. And Earth was but a small blue speck in the cosmic sea.

ABOUT THE AUTHOR

D r. Ronald L. Breazeale received his doctorate in clinical psychology from the University of Tennessee in 1974. He is a clinical psychologist with over 30 years of experience in the fields of mental health and alcohol and drug abuse. Dr. Breazeale has developed and administered numerous mental health and substance abuse programs in hospitals, mental health centers, and independent group practices. These include Criminal Justice Liaison Programs, Emergency Services, and Specialized Outpatient Service Programs. Dr. Breazeale has served as the Executive Director for Psychological and Educational Services, the most extensive independent group mental health and substance abuse practice in Northern New England. He has been active in the field of professional psychology, serving as President of the Maine Psychological Association, and was instrumental in the formation of the Maine Division of Independent Practice. He has served on the Council of Representatives of the American Psychological Association and was involved in the establishment of the APA's Psychology Rural Health Interest Group.

Dr. Breazeale has worked with public safety organizations in some capacity since the mid-1970s. He assisted in the development of a program for public safety supervisors and managers to recognize employee issues and problems and devise strategies to address them before they become significant concerns. This program was taught by the Carolinas Institute for Community Policing, a project funded by the Department of Justice, Office of Community Oriented Policing, and Washington, D.C. His current project, "Maine Resilience: Teaching 21ˢ Century Survival Skills" collaborates with the American Red Cross of Maine, Emergency Management Agencies, and Alpha One.

Resilience is a primary focus area for Dr. Breazeale. Resilience training can assist anyone who must manage crises in life and more effectively deal with everyday stressful situations. Website: http://www.building- resilience.com

Dr. Breazeale has authored a series of novels that addresses conquering fear, building resilience, and bouncing back from adversity. *Reaching Home*, *First Night*, and *Starjacked* have become the core materials that he and his colleagues in Building Resilience use in their resilience training programs. He was instrumental in developing *BounceBack*, a serious game that serves as a training tool for teaching resilience skills.

Areas of consultation expertise for Dr. Breazeale include crisis intervention and management, assessment and management of potentially violent situations, public safety psychology, rural healthcare, managed care system development, and the management of disabling illnesses and chronic conditions. He is currently working with PocketConfidant AI as it develops and uses artificial intelligence to provide resilience coaching.

Reaching Home explores the world he experienced growing up in the "Atomic City" of Oak Ridge, Tennessee as a child with a birth defect. He has worn a prosthetic hook for most of his life.

He is married and has one child, a daughter. Dr. Breazeale now lives and works in southern Maine.

www.ingramcontent.com/pod-product-compliance
Lightning Source LLC
Chambersburg PA
CBHW051140120626
46547CB00012B/879